Get real with

ROCCO GETS REAL

COOK AT HOME, EVERY DAY

WITH SPECIAL THANKS TO KRIS KUREK

Meredith® Books
Des Moines, Iowa

I dedicate this book to my late grandmother, Anna Maria, who taught me so much about what I do without even realizing it. She showed me how to enjoy the company of other people—and she was as real as it gets: real nice, real loving, real fun, really grateful, and a really, really good cook. She was everything I hope to be. Her memory still serves as the benchmark for what being human means to me.

Meredith Books
1716 Locust Street
Des Moines, Iowa 50309–3023
meredithbooks.com

Printed in the United States of America.

First Edition.
Library of Congress Control Number: 2008926650
ISBN: 978-0-696-238-23-9

CONTENTS

> **"** My desire to help **REAL PEOPLE COOK** remains unchanged. My process is more refined now. With each book, I make new discoveries. **"**

Good food fills a lot of needs—the most obvious is satisfying hunger. However, a good meal, whether it takes hours or minutes to make, does more than meet our simplest needs. It satisfies the need we all have to slow down, even for a little while, and connect with the people we care about.

That's where getting real comes in.

As in my last book, *Rocco's Real Life Recipes: Fast Flavor for Every Day*, these new recipes use easy-to-find ingredients. The recipes have short cooking times (most less than 30 minutes) and make minimal mess (one or two pans at the most). And, as always, my strategy is to use a combination of fresh and prepared foods to create recipes that fit into our busy lifestyles but satisfy our increasingly sophisticated tastes.

In cooking—as in any art form, whether it has a practical application or not—there is an element of exploration. In *5-Minute Flavor*, I took the notion of quick and easy cooking to the extreme. In *Rocco's Real Life Recipes*, I relaxed those parameters a little bit. In this book, I come closer to who I am as a chef.

Don't get me wrong—all 140 recipes are still really easy to pull off. There is, however, a level of complexity—whether it's in a flavor profile or a technique—that makes them a little more interesting.

My process is more refined now, and as I write each book, I make new discoveries. There are new products and ideas constantly being developed; the way I integrate them into recipes is being honed and refined.

My desire to help people cook

every day remains unchanged. In that sense, this book is similar to my previous books. I've added a few things, though, one of which relates directly to that desire.

The recipes marked with [TV] come from episodes of either NBC's *The Biggest Loser*™ or *Rocco Gets Real*®, my new show on A&E where I learn about people's real lives and help them get through a milestone event like an engagement by developing the perfect menu and showing them how to make it themselves.

Other new features in the book include:

Eat Healthy: This chapter features recipes I developed for *The Biggest Loser*, as well as some lighter, completely original dishes.

Holidays: These recipes are a combination of my Italian-American family favorites and other special celebratory dishes I've picked up/created along the way. Some of them are quick and easy, but most are a little more elaborate than the bulk of the book, which is intended for everyday cooking.

Writing the book *Rocco Gets Real* is similar to what I get to do on the television show *Rocco Gets Real*. It's an incredibly satisfying privilege. I'm in real people's homes, helping them do something they didn't think they could: become fully empowered cooks.

Enjoy!

Rocco

Irish girl and newbie cook Maggie (maiden name, McFeely) Silvestri married into an Italian family—and wanted to learn how to make homemade macaroni and cheese for her high school-sweetheart husband.

HOW TO USE THIS BOOK

As in my last book, *Rocco's Real Life Recipes,* I've provided some help to make weekday shopping and cooking easy.

Grocery Lists

Every recipe comes with a grocery list that lays out the ingredients—including package sizes— you need to make it. The list is divided into three categories of ingredients:

Fresh: This is anything you get (usually from behind a counter or in the produce section) that's not packaged in a factory and that should be used immediately. It includes vegetables, fruits, fresh herbs, salad greens, meat, poultry, fish and shellfish, and short-storing cheeses, such as ricotta.

Packaged: If it comes in a bag, box, can, carton, jar, or bottle, it likely falls in this category. It includes things like dry pasta, rice, pasta sauces, slightly more esoteric condiments (such as curry paste), cans of crabmeat, and jars of marinated artichoke hearts.

Staples: This is the stuff you should always have around. Staples are things that make an appearance in most recipes, in some combination or form, such as salt and pepper (whole, for grinding fresh), dried herbs and spices, oils and vinegars, butter, eggs, lemons, limes, chicken broth, and long-storing grating cheeses such as Parmigiano-Reggiano.

The Tools Bar

With very rare exception, the recipes in this book require only the most basic cookware. The tools bar shows you the primary pot or pan you'll need to make the recipe. At a glance, you can see if you have it and what you'll have to scrub. I don't like to do a lot of cleanup after a great meal and some wine—I'm pretty sure you don't, either, so I've kept cookware requirements to a minimum. In the instances where the method calls for open-flame cooking (or some semblance of it), I give options of a grill/grill pan/broiler. They're in that order because cooking on a grill gives foods the best flavor—and it's really the easiest too. A grill pan makes a good substitute, but if you don't have one, the broiler works just fine. And in some cases, the broiler really is the best option.

Wine Guide

Food tastes better when enjoyed with a glass of wine. To that end, the wine guide that starts on page 223 matches every recipe in the book (with the exception of those in the Holiday chapter) with what I think is a high-quality, good-value wine that draws out the food's best qualities and rounds out the meal.

The "Fix"

All cooks, no matter how skilled, are somewhere on a learning curve. Occasionally, something doesn't turn out quite the way the cook expected. On the *Rocco Gets Real* recipes, I describe what I did to help the cook in question. On others, I offer up a help for commonly made mistakes. In either case, "The Fix" makes the recipe work—even if it doesn't end up the way it started out. (And that's OK—it's all good.) Here and there, you'll also find "The Assist," which is simply a salient tip to help shopping and/or cooking go more smoothly.

The Biggest Loser Guidelines

These recipes really put my creativity to the test. I never want to sacrifice flavor (it's the most important thing when it comes to enjoying food), but I was charged with the challenge of creating contestants' favorite dishes observing the following guidelines:

- Ingredients must be all-natural.
- No sugar allowed.
- Little or no fat or sodium allowed.
- No modified-starch carbs allowed.
- Each serving is 350 calories or less.
- Ingredients cost $7 or less for four servings.

The results surprised even me, in a good way.

❝ BEEF no longer gets the bad rap it used to. I'm a big fan of good old red meat. To me, there's nothing like a perfectly charred steak. ❞

GRILLED **BEEF** TENDERLOIN & PINEAPPLE AU POIVRE WITH COCONUT SAUCE

Look for cored and peeled fresh pineapple in the produce section of your supermarket to save the time it takes to carve a whole pineapple. **makes 4 servings**

ingredients

1½ pounds beef tenderloin, cut into four 6-ounce portions, about 1 inch thick
  Salt
2 tablespoons coarsely ground black peppercorns
1 cored fresh pineapple, cut into ¾-inch-thick rings, juice reserved
  Freshly ground pepper
1 13.5-ounce can coconut milk
3 tablespoons fish sauce
½ cup unsweetened coconut flakes, toasted
1 bunch scallions, sliced thin on a bias (see how-to, page 21)

method

1. Heat a grill/grill pan/broiler over high heat. Season steaks with salt and press one side of the meat into the peppercorns so that the surface is completely covered. Place steaks on the grill, pepper side down, and cook 2 to 3 minutes per side for medium rare. Remove from grill. Cover lightly with foil to keep warm.
2. Season pineapple with salt and pepper. Grill until lightly charred, 3 to 4 minutes per side.
3. Meanwhile, heat reserved pineapple juice and coconut milk in a medium saucepan over medium-high heat. Cook until reduced to a sauce consistency, about 6 minutes. Add fish sauce. Season with salt and pepper to taste; stir in toasted coconut.
4. Overlap steaks and pineapple slices on a platter. Spoon the coconut sauce evenly over all, and scatter scallions on top.

grocery list

fresh

1½ pounds beef tenderloin

1 fresh pineapple

1 bunch scallions

packaged

13.5-ounce can
coconut milk

7-ounce jar fish sauce

12-ounce package
unsweetened coconut
flakes

tools

grill pan

medium saucepan

BARBECUE ROAST **BEEF** WITH CORN & BEANS

Steer clear of the overcooked casseroles and heavy-on-the-mayo salads at the counter of the supermarket deli; fortunately, it's also got a wealth of foods that can be the foundation of a great homemade dish. Fresh, rare-roasted beef is one of them. **makes 4 servings**

grocery list

fresh

6 slices bacon

1¼ pounds sliced rare roast beef

1 bunch scallions

packaged

10-ounce package frozen corn

15-ounce can black beans

4-ounce jar pimientos

18-ounce bottle barbecue sauce

12-ounce package English muffins

tools

large sauté pan

ingredients

6   slices bacon, cut into large dice

1½ cups frozen corn

1   15-ounce can black beans, rinsed and drained

1   cup bottled diced pimientos

1½ cups barbecue sauce, preferably a sweet and sour sauce

1¼ pounds sliced rare roast beef, cut into 1-inch-wide strips

1   large bunch scallions, sliced thin on a bias (see how-to photos, page 21)

Salt and freshly ground pepper

4   English muffins

method

1. Heat a large sauté pan over medium-high heat. When pan is hot, add the bacon and cook, stirring occasionally, for about 2 minutes, or until fat begins to render. Add the corn, beans, pimientos, and barbecue sauce to the pan. Simmer until vegetables are hot, about 3 minutes. Add roast beef to pan and stir until it is completely coated with sauce. Continue to cook just until beef is warm, about 2 minutes. Add scallions and season with salt and pepper to taste.
2. Meanwhile, toast the English muffins. To serve, spoon beef mixture on top of muffins.

the fix
If you oversauce your meat to the point that it resembles soup, just scoop it into a colander and press out the extra sauce with the back of a spoon.

BEEF TENDERLOIN WITH SWEET & SOUR NAPA CABBAGE

Napa cabbage is easy to prepare and cook, but it has a lot of water in it—so be sure to get the pan really hot before you start cooking. **makes 4 servings**

ingredients

2   tablespoons vegetable oil
1½ pounds filet mignon, cut
    into 4 portions, ¾ to 1 inch
    thick
    Salt and freshly ground
    pepper
1   large head napa cabbage,
    shredded, about 6 cups
1   6-ounce package Sunsweet®
    Orchard Mix Dried Fruit,
    coarsely chopped
½   cup POM Wonderful®
    pomegranate juice
¼   cup Dijon mustard
3   tablespoons chopped fresh
    tarragon

method

1. Heat 1 tablespoon of the oil in a large sauté pan over high heat. Season steaks generously with salt and pepper and add to pan. Cook steaks about 2 minutes per side for rare. Remove steaks from the pan and set aside to rest in a warm place.
2. Add the remaining tablespoon of oil to the pan. Add cabbage to pan. Season with salt and pepper to taste and cook, stirring frequently, until almost tender, about 3 minutes. Add dried fruit and pomegranate juice. Bring to a simmer and cook for about 1 minute or until cabbage is tender. Stir in mustard and tarragon. Season with salt and pepper to taste, if necessary.
3. Serve steaks on a bed of the cabbage mixture.

grocery list

fresh
1½ pounds filet mignon
1 large head napa cabbage

packaged
6-ounce package Sunsweet® Orchard Mix Dried Fruit

16-ounce bottle POM Wonderful® pomegranate juice

1-ounce package fresh tarragon

staples
vegetable oil
Dijon mustard

tools

large sauté pan

BEEF WITH SALSA VERDE, RICE & BEANS

Tomatillos have a great lemony and just-a-little-bit-bracing flavor that really brightens up the rich, meaty taste of beef. **makes 4 servings**

grocery list

fresh

1½ pounds ground beef

1 bunch cilantro

2 ripe avocados

packaged

10-ounce package frozen corn

Two 8.8-ounce packages Uncle Ben's® Original Long-Grain Ready Rice®

15-ounce can black beans

16-ounce jar Desert Pepper® Trading Company Salsa Del Rio

staples

sour cream

tools

large sauté pan

ingredients

1½ pounds ground beef
Salt and freshly ground pepper

1½ cups frozen corn kernels

2 8.8-ounce packages Uncle Ben's® Original Long-Grain Ready Rice®

1 15-ounce can black beans, rinsed and drained

1½ cups tomatillo salsa or green salsa, preferably Desert Pepper® Trading Company Salsa Del Rio

½ cup sour cream

⅔ cup chopped cilantro

2 ripe avocados, sliced (see how-to photos, page 15)

method

1. Heat a large sauté pan over high heat. Add ground beef to pan and season with salt and pepper. Cook, stirring occasionally, for about 3 minutes. Add corn and cook, stirring occasionally, until corn is tender and beef is cooked through, 3 to 4 more minutes.
2. Meanwhile, combine the rice and beans in a medium microwave-safe bowl. Microwave on high for about 3 minutes, or until hot throughout. Season with salt and pepper to taste.
3. Add salsa, sour cream, and cilantro to the beef mixture. Season with salt and pepper to taste. Spoon beef mixture onto a bed of the beans and rice. Top with avocado slices and serve.

3. With a quick, slightly forceful chopping motion bring the blade down onto the seed so the blade sticks into it. Turn the knife about a quarter turn and slowly lift up, pulling the seed up and out of the fruit. To slice the avocado, scoop the exposed half of the fruit out of the skin with a large spoon. You can then easily slice the avocado.

1. Put the avocado in the palm of your hand. Using a large chef's knife, cut lengthwise into the fruit. Turn the avocado all of the way around so the knife glides through, cutting fruit in half.

2. Twist the avocado halves apart so the flesh and seed are exposed.

BROILED ROAST **BEEF** WITH SUN-DRIED TOMATOES & PARMIGIANO ON FLATBREAD

When I say "flatbread," I am really thinking pizza. If it was possible, I'd turn nearly every dish I ate into pizza of some kind. It's a portable meal on a very tasty edible plate. **makes 4 servings**

grocery list

fresh

1¼ pounds rare roast beef, sliced thin

2 small bunches watercress

packaged

14-ounce package Toufayan Mediterranean Style Wheat Flatbread

3.15-ounce tube Amore® garlic paste

7.5-ounce jar sun-dried tomatoes in olive oil

16-ounce jar Italian mix giardiniera

staples

light mayonnaise

Parmigiano-Reggiano cheese

ingredients

4   whole-wheat flatbreads, about 8 inches in diameter
1¼ pounds rare roast beef, sliced thin
1   cup light mayonnaise
1   cup grated Parmigiano-Reggiano cheese
1   teaspoon Amore® garlic paste, or 2 cloves garlic, minced
⅔   cup sun-dried tomatoes in olive oil, drained and roughly chopped
1   cup Italian mix giardiniera (pickled vegetables), roughly chopped
    Salt and freshly ground pepper
2   small bunches watercress, cleaned and dried

method

1. Preheat the broiler on low.
2. Line a rimmed baking sheet with foil and lay flatbreads out on the sheet. Divide roast beef among the flatbreads, completely covering the surface of the bread.
3. In a small bowl, mix together the mayonnaise, cheese, garlic paste, sun-dried tomatoes, and pickled vegetables. Season with salt and pepper to taste. Spread the mixture evenly over the roast beef. Broil until cheese is golden brown and bubbly, about 4 minutes.
4. Divide the watercress evenly among the flatbreads and serve.

tools

rimmed baking sheet

BEEF EGGPLANT & MOZZARELLA CASSEROLE

Caponata is a classic sweet-and-sour Sicilian relish made with fried eggplant, peppers, and often capers and/or olives. It's a great accompaniment to grilled meats and fish. **makes 4 servings**

grocery list

fresh

1½ pounds ground beef

packaged

Two 13.5-ounce pouches Bertolli® Premium Summer Crushed Tomato & Basil pasta sauce

Two 7.5-ounce jars Paesana™ caponata

1-ounce package fresh basil

4-ounce package Eli Zabar® Toasted Parmesan Bread Crisps

8-ounce package shredded mozzarella cheese

tools

large cast-iron skillet

ingredients

1½ pounds ground beef
Salt and freshly ground pepper
2 13.5-ounce pouches Bertolli® Premium Summer Crushed Tomato & Basil pasta sauce (about 3 cups)
2 7.5-ounce jars Paesana caponata
⅓ cup chopped fresh basil
2 cups crushed Parmesan crackers, preferably Eli Zabar® Toasted Parmesan Bread Crisps
½ pound shredded mozzarella or 4-cheese pizza blend

method

1. Preheat the broiler on high.
2. Heat a large cast-iron skillet over high heat. When hot, add the ground beef to the skillet. Season with salt and pepper. Cook, stirring occasionally, until meat is brown and cooked through, about 6 minutes. Drain fat, if necessary. Add pasta sauce and caponata to the pan and bring the mixture to a simmer.
3. Stir basil and Parmesan crackers into the meat mixture. Season with salt and pepper to taste, if necessary. Sprinkle mozzarella evenly on top of meat. Broil until cheese melts, about 4 minutes.

GROUND **BEEF** WITH RED CABBAGE & SOUR CREAM

This is just the kind of thing I want to eat on a cool fall night. The flavors and textures—hearty brown and wild rice, sour cream, and sweet-and-sour red cabbage—just taste of that time of year.

makes 4 servings

ingredients

2   8.8-ounce packages Uncle Ben's® Brown and Wild Ready Rice®
    Salt and freshly ground pepper
1½ pounds ground beef
1   16-ounce jar sweet and sour red cabbage preferably Greenwood® drained
½   cup chopped fresh parsley
1½ cups sour cream

method

1. Empty rice into a medium bowl and season to taste with salt and pepper. Cover with plastic wrap and microwave until hot, 3 to 4 minutes.

2. Meanwhile, heat a large sauté pan over high heat. When it's hot, add the ground beef. Season with salt and pepper and cook until brown and just cooked through, about 6 minutes. Drain fat, if necessary. Add cabbage and cook for another 3 minutes, or until cabbage is hot. Turn off the heat and stir in parsley and sour cream. Season to taste with salt and pepper, if necessary. Spoon beef and cabbage mixture over rice and serve.

grocery list

fresh

1½ pounds ground beef

packaged

Two 8.8-ounce packages Uncle Ben's® Brown and Wild Ready Rice®

16-ounce jar Greenwood® sweet and sour red cabbage

1-ounce package fresh parsley

staples

sour cream

tools

large sauté pan

ROAST **BEEF** WITH TERIYAKI RICE NOODLES & SCALLIONS

Wide rice noodles are commonly used in both Chinese and Thai cooking. They bring a great bite—a hearty, toothsome texture—to this dish. **makes 4 servings**

grocery list

fresh

6-inch piece of ginger

1 pound sliced rare roast beef

1 bunch scallions

packaged

Two 6-ounce packages wide rice noodles

12-ounce package sliced red bell peppers

Two 11-ounce bottles House of Tsang® Korean Teriyaki stir-fry sauce

staples

toasted sesame oil

tools

stockpot

large sauté pan

ingredients

¾ pound wide rice noodles
  Salt and freshly ground pepper

2 tablespoons toasted sesame oil

2 tablespoons chopped fresh ginger

1 12-ounce package sliced red bell peppers or 2 medium red bell peppers, stemmed, seeded, and sliced

1½ 11-ounce bottles House of Tsang® Korean Teriyaki stir-fry sauce (about 2 cups)

1 pound sliced rare roast beef, cut into ribbons about ¼ inch wide

1 bunch scallions, thinly sliced on a bias (see how-to photos, page 21)

method

1. Bring a stockpot of salted water to a boil. Cook noodles according to package directions. Drain.
2. Meanwhile, in a large sauté pan, heat sesame oil over medium heat. Add ginger and red peppers and sauté until peppers are tender, about 3 to 4 minutes. Add sauce to the pan and bring to a simmer. Add beef and continue to cook until beef is warm. Toss beef and sauce mixture with the noodles and scallions. Season to taste with salt and pepper, if necessary.

1. Cutting on a bias means to cut on an angle. It makes foods like scallions or carrots look more attractive. Place a few scallions on a cutting board. Hold your knife at a 45° angle across the top of them and begin slicing.

2. The result you get isn't tubular but a little pointed—like penne pasta. Continue slicing through, adjusting the angle of your knife to determine just how angled you would like the pieces to be.

FILET MIGNON WITH EGGPLANT IN TANGY TOMATO-YOGURT SAUCE

Yogurt is one of my go-to sauce bases. It's thick, creamy, and has acidity that blends well with richer flavors. Fage® brand of Greek yogurt is of noticeably higher quality than others. **makes 4 servings**

grocery list

fresh

1¼ pounds filet mignon

1 bunch scallions

packaged

Two 8.8-ounce packages Uncle Ben's® Original Long-Grain Ready Rice®

15-ounce can Progresso® chickpeas

14-ounce container Sabra® Go Mediterranean® sautéed eggplant in tangy tomato sauce

17.6-ounce container Fage® Total Greek yogurt

staples

vegetable oil

tools

large sauté pan

ingredients

2   8.8-ounce packages Uncle Ben's® Original Long Grain Ready Rice®

1   15-ounce can Progresso® chickpeas, rinsed and drained
    Salt and freshly ground pepper

2   tablespoons vegetable oil

1¼ pounds filet mignon, cut into bite-size cubes

1   14-ounce container Sabra® Go Mediterranean® sautéed eggplant in tangy tomato sauce

1   cup Greek yogurt, preferably Fage®

1   bunch scallions, sliced thin on a bias (see how-to photos, page 21)

method

1. In a medium microwave-safe bowl, combine rice and chickpeas. Season with salt and pepper to taste. Cover with plastic wrap and microwave on high for 3 to 4 minutes, or until hot throughout.
2. Meanwhile, heat oil in a large sauté pan over high heat. Season meat with salt and pepper and add to pan. Cook, stirring occasionally, until meat is brown but still rare in the center, about 5 minutes. Remove meat from the pan. Add eggplant to the pan. Bring to a boil, turn off the heat, and add steak back to the pan. Stir in the yogurt and scallions. Season with salt and pepper to taste.
3. Spoon the steak-eggplant mixture over a bed of the rice and chickpeas.

TINY **MEATBALLS** & TORTELLINI WITH BROCCOLI RABE
Yes, I am using frozen prepared meatballs in this recipe. Please don't tell my Mom!
makes 4 servings

ingredients

1 pound frozen mini meatballs
Salt and freshly ground
  pepper
2 13.5-ounce pouches Bertolli®
  Premium Summer Crushed
  Tomato & Basil pasta sauce
  (about 3 cups)
1 16-ounce package
  refrigerated cheese
  tortellini
1 bunch broccoli rabe, roughly
  chopped
⅓ cup fresh chopped basil
1 cup freshly grated
  Parmigiano-Reggiano
  cheese

method

1. Bring a stockpot of salted water to a boil. Meanwhile, microwave meatballs in a large bowl until hot, according to package instructions. Add pasta sauce to bowl, cover with plastic, and continue to microwave until sauce is hot, about 3 more minutes.
2. Meanwhile, cook the tortellini according to package instructions. About halfway through the cooking time, add broccoli rabe to the water. Continue to cook until tortellini are done and broccoli rabe is tender, about 3 minutes. Drain.
3. Toss tortellini and broccoli rabe with the meatballs, sauce, and basil.
4. Top with cheese and serve.

grocery list

fresh
1 bunch broccoli rabe

packaged
1 pound frozen mini
meatballs

Two 13.5-ounce pouches
Bertolli® Premium
Summer Crushed Tomato
& Basil pasta sauce

16-ounce package
refrigerated cheese
tortellini

1-ounce package fresh
basil

staples
Parmigiano-Reggiano
cheese

tools

stockpot

CHOPPED **STEAK** WITH CHARRED ONIONS & QUESO BLANCO

Queso blanco is Spanish for white cheese. It's wonderful to cook with because unlike most American-style cheeses, it becomes soft and creamy when heated but won't melt.

makes 4 servings

grocery list

fresh

1¼ pounds ground beef

1 bunch cilantro

packaged

16-ounce jar Salpica®
Cilantro Green Olive Salsa
with Roasted Tomatillos

8-ounce package queso
blanco

staples

Vidalia onions

eggs

capers

extra-virgin olive oil

tools

grill pan

ingredients

2 small Vidalia or red onions,
   sliced into ½-inch-thick
   rings
   Bertolli® extra-virgin olive
   oil
   Salt and freshly ground
   pepper
4 ground beef patties,
   1 to 1¼ pounds total
4 hard-boiled eggs, chopped
1 16-ounce jar Salpica®
   Cilantro Green Olive Salsa
   with Roasted Tomatillos, or
   salsa verde of choice
3 tablespoons capers
6 ounces queso blanco,
   crumbled
½ cup chopped fresh cilantro
2 tablespoons Bertolli® extra-
   virgin olive oil

method

1. Heat a grill/grill pan/broiler
on high.
2. Brush both sides of onion slices
with olive oil. Season with salt and
pepper and place on grill. When
one side is charred, after about
5 minutes, turn onion slices over.
3. Season beef patties with salt
and pepper. Place on grill next
to onions and cook for about
2½ minutes per side for medium-
rare. Remove patties and onions
from grill. Onions should be
tender and nicely charred on
both sides.
4. Meanwhile, in a medium bowl
combine eggs with salsa, capers,
cheese, and cilantro. Stir in olive
oil and season with salt and
pepper to taste.
5. Pile one-quarter of the onions
on top of each patty. Top with
salsa mixture and serve.

1. Using a sharp knife, cut the tops and bottoms off of the onions. Carefully remove peels and discard. Using the knife, cut each onion into large ½-inch-thick rings.

2. Place onion slices on a plate. Using a pastry brush, brush olive oil evenly over both sides of onion slices. Sprinkle lightly with salt and freshly ground black pepper.

3. Meanwhile, if cooking in a grill pan, heat the pan over high heat. Place onion slices in the pan and cook until the onions are charred, turning once.

BEEF WELLINGTON

I devised this version of the old-school classic for Rob Capobianco. He was in the doghouse with his girlfriend because he didn't propose when she thought he should have. He thought Beef Wellington would impress her, especially if he proposed during dinner. It did. She said yes. **makes 2 servings**

ingredients

2 tablespoons vegetable oil
1 2½ -pound piece beef tenderloin
   Salt and freshly ground pepper
1 17.5-ounce package frozen puff pastry, thawed
6 ounces duck foie gras mousse, preferably D'Artagnan®
1 egg, lightly beaten
2 tablespoons butter
8 ounces sliced mixed mushrooms
⅔ cup dry red wine
1 18-ounce can Progresso® Creamy Mushroom Soup
¼ cup chopped flat-leaf parsley

method

1. Preheat oven to 425°F. Line a baking sheet with parchment paper.

2. In a large cast-iron skillet heat oil over high heat. When oil is smoking, season beef generously with salt and pepper. Add to pan and brown meat on all sides. Remove meat from pan; cool slightly.

3. Lay one sheet of puff pastry on a work surface. Spread the center of the pastry with about half the pâté. Place beef on top of pâté; spread beef with remaining pâté.

4. In a small bowl combine the egg with 1 tablespoon cold water to make an egg wash. Brush edges of pastry surrounding the beef lightly with the egg wash. Lay the remaining piece of pastry on top of the beef. Gently press the pastry to conform to the shape of the beef. Press the edges of the pastry firmly to seal. Cut away all but about a 1½-inch border of pastry surrounding the beef. Crimp the edges in a decorative pattern. Transfer to the prepared baking sheet and refrigerate for about 10 minutes.

5. Remove from refrigerator and brush entire surface of pastry with egg wash. Bake for about 30 minutes for medium-rare. Allow to rest 7 minutes before slicing.

6. Meanwhile, wipe out pan beef was cooked in. Add butter to pan and let melt over medium heat. Add the mushrooms and cook until tender, about 5 minutes. Add the wine to the pan and stir, scraping the bottom of the pan to loosen any flavorful brown bits. Cook, stirring occasionally, for about 8 minutes.

7. Add the soup to the pan and simmer until a sauce consistency is achieved, about 3 minutes. Season to taste with salt and pepper; stir in the parsley.

8. To serve, spoon mushroom sauce over slices of beef.

the fix

Rob overcooked the beef a little bit and it kinda fell apart when he tried to slice it. So I took the contents, diced it up, and made a potpie out of it. I used some of the pastry scraps to write "Will you marry me?" on the top. And that's how he got engaged.

CURRIED GROUND **BEEF** & NOODLE STEW WITH ZUCCHINI

There are lots of prepared Asian sauces out there, but unfortunately most are not so good. Ironically the most complex of them—the Thai sauces—seem able to hang most authentically with the homemade sauces. Take advantage of it. **makes 4 servings**

ingredients

2   14-ounce cans chicken broth
2   7-ounce pouches Blue
    Dragon® Royal Thai Red
    Curry Cooking Sauce
    Salt and freshly ground
    pepper
1   pound ground beef
1   5-ounce package Japanese
    curly noodles
2   small zucchini, cut in half
    horizontally and sliced thin
    (about 3 cups)
    Juice of 2 limes
⅔   cup chopped fresh cilantro
½   cup slivered almonds,
    toasted

method

1. In a large saucepan, bring chicken broth and curry sauce to a boil. Season broth with salt and pepper to taste.
2. Break meat into small chunks and add to the broth. Stir in noodles and zucchini. Cook, stirring occasionally, for about 5 minutes, or until noodles are tender and meat is cooked through.
3. Add lime juice and cilantro. Season with salt and pepper to taste, if necessary. Ladle into bowls and sprinkle almonds on top.

grocery list

fresh

1 pound ground beef

2 small zucchini

1 bunch cilantro

packaged

Two 7-ounce pouches Blue Dragon® Royal Thai Red Curry Cooking Sauce

5-ounce package Japanese curly noodles

2-ounce package slivered almonds

staples

chicken broth

limes

tools

large saucepan

GINGERED **BEEF** STEW WITH BOK CHOY & SHIITAKE MUSHROOMS

Shiitake mushrooms have a meatiness and intense flavor that bring tremendous depth to a dish. Remove the stems—they're really fibrous and would be pretty unpleasant to eat. **makes 4 servings**

grocery list

fresh

1 pound filet mignon

6-inch piece of ginger

8 ounces shiitake mushrooms

1 head bok choy

1 bunch scallions

packaged

8-ounce jar chili oil

10-ounce bottle Kikkoman® ponzu sauce

staples

chicken broth

tools

large saucepan

ingredients

2   tablespoons chili oil
2   tablespoons chopped fresh ginger
8   ounces shiitake mushrooms, stems removed, thinly sliced
5   cups thinly sliced bok choy
2   14-ounce cans chicken broth
¾   cup Kikkoman® ponzu sauce
1   pound filet mignon, sliced thin
    Salt and freshly ground pepper
1   bunch scallions, sliced thin on a bias (see how-to photos, page 21)

method

1. In a large saucepan, heat chili oil over high heat. Add ginger and sauté for 1 minute. Add mushrooms and continue to cook for another 3 minutes, stirring occasionally. Add bok choy and cook for another 3 minutes. Add chicken broth and ponzu sauce. Bring mixture to a simmer.
2. When bok choy is tender (about 4 minutes), turn heat to low. Season filet with salt and pepper and add to broth. Lightly poach the beef in the broth until just rare, about 2 minutes. Stir in scallions. Season with salt and pepper to taste, if necessary.

GRILLED **BEEF** TENDERLOIN WITH NOODLES, CASHEWS & CHILI SAUCE

Cashew nuts were very popular when I was a kid, but macadamias eclipsed them—I never understood why. Cashews have a sweet, mellow, sophisticated flavor at half the price. **makes 4 servings**

ingredients

2   5-ounce packages Ka-Me®
    Japanese curly noodles
5   tablespoons Kikkoman®
    Thai-style chili sauce
1½ pounds filet mignon, cut into
    four 6-ounce portions,
    about 1 inch thick
    Salt and freshly ground
    pepper
2   tablespoons fish sauce
3   tablespoons toasted sesame
    oil
    Juice of 2 limes
1   4.5-ounce package toasted
    salted cashews, crushed
1   bunch scallions, sliced thin
    on a bias (see how-to
    photos, page 21)

method

1. Bring a stockpot of salted water to a boil. Cook noodles according to package directions. Drain.
2. Meanwhile, preheat grill/grill pan/broiler on high. Rub 2 tablespoons of the chili sauce into the meat and season generously with salt and pepper. Grill about 3 minutes per side for medium rare. Let rest 5 minutes, then slice thin, if desired.
3. Toss cooked noodles with fish sauce, sesame oil, lime juice, cashews, scallions and remaining 3 tablespoons chili sauce. Season to taste with salt and pepper. Lay a bed of noodles on a serving platter and arrange beef on top.

grocery list

fresh

1½ pounds filet mignon

1 bunch scallions

packaged

Two 5-ounce packages
Ka-Me® Japanese curly
noodles

9-ounce jar Kikkoman®
Thai-style chili sauce

7-ounce jar fish sauce

4.5-ounce package salted
cashews

staples

toasted sesame oil

limes

tools

grill pan

stockpot

LARGE **MEATBALLS** WITH CHERRY PEPPERS & POTATOES

These meatballs are gorgeous, and because they're large—about 4 ounces each—you don't have to roll many of them. The combination of the fiery, vinegary cherry peppers and the sweet tomato sauce makes for a great-tasting, well-balanced sauce. **makes 4 servings**

ingredients

1½ pounds ground beef
⅓ cup plain breadcrumbs
½ cup freshly grated Parmigiano-Reggiano cheese
2 eggs, beaten well
1 teaspoon salt, plus more for seasoning
½ teaspoon freshly ground black pepper, plus more for seasoning
1 large Idaho potato
2 13.5-ounce pouches Bertolli® Premium Champignon and Portobello Mushroom pasta sauce (about 3 cups)
½ cup sliced hot cherry peppers, drained
½ cup chopped fresh flat-leaf parsley or fresh basil

method

1. Preheat the oven to 375°F. In a large bowl, mix together the ground beef, breadcrumbs, cheese, eggs, 1 teaspoon salt, and ½ teaspoon pepper. Divide mixture into 8 portions. Roll each portion into a large meatball.
2. Peel the potato and shred it on a box grater. Wrap the shredded potato in a clean cotton kitchen towel. Hold it over the sink and squeeze as much water out of the potatoes as you can.
3. Combine the pasta sauce and cherry peppers in a medium microwave-safe bowl. Cover with plastic wrap and microwave on high until hot, 3 to 4 minutes. Stir in shredded potatoes. Season generously with salt and pepper.
4. Pour the pasta sauce mixture in a 9x13-inch baking dish. Add the meatballs to the pan and season with salt and pepper. Cover with aluminum foil and bake for about 30 minutes. Turn each meatball over. Continue to bake until meatballs are cooked through and potatoes are tender, another 20 to 30 minutes.
5. Sprinkle parsley on top and serve.

grocery list

fresh
1½ pounds ground beef
1 large Idaho potato

packaged
Two 13.5-ounce pouches Bertolli® Premium Champignon and Portobello Mushroom pasta sauce
16-ounce bottle sliced hot cherry peppers
1 bunch fresh flat-leaf parsley or basil

staples
Plain breadcrumbs
Parmigiano-Reggiano cheese
eggs

tools
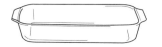
9×13-inch baking dish

GRILLED **RIBEYE** WITH WARM THAI PEANUT, CARROT & SNOW PEA SLAW

Ribeye is the juiciest cut of beef, so it really doesn't need a rich garnish. Crunchy, brightly flavored carrots and snow peas tossed with a little bit of peanut sauce are perfect. **makes 4 servings**

grocery list

fresh

1½ pounds ribeye

1 bunch cilantro

packaged

10-ounce package shredded carrots

6-ounce package fresh snow peas

11.5-ounce bottle House of Tsang® Bangkok Padang peanut sauce

staples

toasted sesame oil

light mayonnaise

tools

grill pan

large sauté pan

ingredients

1½ pounds ribeye, cut into four, 6-ounce portions, about 1 inch thick

Salt and freshly ground pepper

1 tablespoon toasted sesame oil

1 10-ounce package shredded carrots

1 6-ounce package fresh snow peas

⅓ cup light mayonnaise

½ cup House of Tsang® Bangkok Padang peanut sauce

⅔ cup chopped fresh cilantro

method

1. Preheat grill/grill pan/broiler on high. Season steaks with salt and pepper. Grill about 3 minutes per side for medium rare. Remove from grill and allow to rest.

2. While steak is cooking, heat sesame oil in a large sauté pan over high heat. When oil is hot, add the shredded carrots and snow peas to the pan. Sauté, tossing or stirring occasionally, until vegetables are warm and beginning to wilt but still have crunch, about 3 minutes.

3. Meanwhile, make the dressing: In a large bowl, whisk together the mayonnaise and peanut sauce. Add the warm carrots and snow peas to the bowl, along with the cilantro. Toss and season to taste with salt and pepper.

4. Transfer slaw to a large platter. Lay steaks on top of the slaw and serve immediately.

GRILLED **STEAK** & ROMAINE WITH PEPPERS & OLIVES

The idea here was to extrapolate one of my favorite snacks—Parmesan crisps—into a meal.
(So I had to add a few things.) **makes 4 servings**

ingredients

1½ pounds filet mignon, cut into 4 portions, about ¾ inch thick

½ cup creamy Caesar dressing, preferably Marie's®
    Salt and freshly ground pepper

2 hearts of romaine lettuce, ends trimmed, split in half lengthwise

⅓ cup pitted mixed Mediterranean olives, chopped

½ cup Mancini® roasted red pepper strips

1 cup Parmesan crackers, preferably Eli Zabar® Toasted Parmesan Bread Crisps, crushed into small pieces

¼ cup chopped fresh basil

method

1. Heat a grill/grill pan/broiler on high. Lightly brush steaks with 1 to 2 tablespoons of the dressing. Season with salt and pepper. Grill about 2 minutes per side for medium rare. Remove steaks from grill and allow to rest.
2. Place hearts of romaine on the grill, cut side down. Grill until slightly charred and warm but not cooked, about 1 minute per side.
3. Meanwhile, mix the remaining dressing with the olives, peppers, crackers, basil, and any juices that may have accumulated from the steak as it rested.
4. Lay the lettuce on a large serving platter, cut side up. Lay one steak on top of each heart of romaine half. Spoon the olive mixture over the top and serve.

grocery list

fresh

1½ pounds filet mignon

2 hearts of romaine lettuce

packaged

12-ounce jar Marie's® Caesar salad dressing

12-ounce jar mixed Mediterranean olives

10-ounce can Mancini® roasted red pepper strips

4-ounce box Eli Zabar® Toasted Parmesan Bread Crisps

1-ounce package fresh basil

tools

grill pan

MOROCCAN **BEEF** STEW

In Morocco, there's no fear of big, bold flavors. If you can find the fiery Moroccan condiment known as harissa, add some to the finished stew. **makes 4 servings**

grocery list

fresh

1¼ pounds filet mignon

1 bunch cilantro

packaged

10-ounce box couscous

1-pound package mustard greens

Two 7-ounce containers Sabra® Moroccan Matbucha

staples

vegetable oil

low-sodium chicken broth

cayenne pepper

tools

medium saucepan

large cast-iron skillet

ingredients

2 cups water
1½ cups couscous
2 tablespoons vegetable oil
1¼ pounds filet mignon, cut into bite-size chunks
Salt and freshly ground pepper
5 cups cleaned mustard greens, roughly chopped
2 7-ounce containers Sabra® Moroccan Matbucha, or 1¾ cups of your favorite salsa
1 cup low-sodium chicken broth
¼ teaspoon cayenne pepper
½ cup chopped fresh cilantro

method

1. In a medium saucepan, bring water to boiling. Turn off the heat. Stir in the couscous and cover. Set aside.

2. Meanwhile, heat oil in a large cast-iron skillet. Season meat generously with salt and pepper. Carefully add meat to pan and sauté, stirring occasionally, until meat is evenly brown and cooked to medium rare, about 4 minutes. Remove meat from pan.

3. Add mustard greens to pan and cook, stirring often, until wilted, about 3 minutes. Season to taste with salt and pepper. Stir in matbucha, chicken broth, and cayenne. Continue to cook, stirring occasionally, until the mixture is hot, about 2 more minutes. Return beef to pan. Season to taste with salt and black pepper, if necessary. Stir in cilantro.

4. Fluff the couscous with a fork. Make a bed of the couscous on a platter and spoon beef mixture on top.

GROUND **BEEF** STEAKS WITH MUSHROOMS & HONEY-MUSTARD EGGPLANT

Maille®-brand Dijon may not be as familiar as that other, more widely known Dijon, but it consistently wins competitions. It also comes infused with herbs, spices, and green peppercorns. **makes 4 servings**

grocery list

fresh

1¼ pounds ground beef

1 bunch flat-leaf parsley

packaged

8-ounce package white button mushrooms

12-ounce jar marinated eggplant strips

8-ounce jar Maille® honey Dijon mustard

staples

extra-virgin olive oil

tools

rimmed baking sheet

medium saucepan

ingredients

3 tablespoons Bertolli® extra-virgin olive oil

4 ground beef patties, 1 to 1¼ pounds total
Salt and freshly ground pepper

1 8-ounce package sliced white button mushrooms
Water

1 12-ounce jar marinated eggplant strips, drained

1 8-ounce jar honey mustard, preferably Maille® honey Dijon

½ cup chopped fresh flat-leaf parsley

method

1. Preheat broiler on high. Line a rimmed baking sheet with foil and coat lightly with 1 tablespoon of the olive oil. Place ground beef patties on baking sheet and season with salt and pepper.

2. In a medium bowl, toss the mushrooms with the remaining olive oil and season generously with salt and pepper. Pile one fourth of the mushrooms on top of each patty. Broil until beef is cooked through and mushrooms are slightly browned, about 6 minutes. Pour accumulated cooking juices into a measuring cup. Add enough water to equal ½ cup.

3. Meanwhile, heat eggplant and honey mustard in a medium saucepan over medium heat. Add the reserved cooking liquid/water to the eggplant mixture and bring to a simmer. Stir in parsley. Spoon eggplant mixture over each beef patty and serve.

GROUND **BEEF** WITH CAULIFLOWER CURRY & RICE

If you think it's difficult to pull off an authentic-tasting Indian curry, Patak's Curry Paste will make you feel like a native of Bombay. It's intensely flavored and wildly, wonderfully aromatic.

makes 4 servings

ingredients

1½ 10-ounce packages frozen cauliflower florets (about 4 cups)

2 8.8-ounce packages Uncle Ben's® Vegetable Harvest Ready Whole Grain Medley™
Salt and freshly ground pepper

1¼ pounds ground beef

3 tablespoons Patak's® mild curry paste

2 13.5-ounce pouches Bertolli® Premium Champignon and Portobello Mushroom pasta sauce (about 3 cups)

½ cup chopped fresh mint

method

1. Put cauliflower in a medium microwaveable bowl and cover with plastic wrap. Microwave on high until warm, 3 to 4 minutes. Set aside.

2. Empty contents of Ready Rice packages in another medium microwave-safe bowl. Season to taste with salt and pepper, if necessary. Cover with plastic wrap and microwave on high until hot, 3 to 4 minutes.

3. Meanwhile, heat a large cast-iron skillet over high heat. When hot, add beef. Season with salt and pepper. Cook, stirring occasionally, until beef begins to brown, about 5 minutes. Add curry paste, pasta sauce, and cauliflower. Stir to combine. Simmer until beef is cooked through and cauliflower is hot, about 3 more minutes.

4. Stir in mint. Season to taste with salt and pepper, if necessary. Serve curry mixture over rice.

grocery list

fresh

1¼ pounds ground beef

packaged

Two 10-ounce packages frozen cauliflower florets

Two 8.8-ounce packages Uncle Ben's® Vegetable Harvest Ready Whole Grain Medley™

10-ounce jar Patak's® mild curry paste

Two 13.5-ounce pouches Bertolli® Premium Champignon and Portobello Mushroom pasta sauce

1 bunch fresh mint

tools

large cast-iron skillet

SAUTÉED **BEEF** TENDERLOIN WITH APRICOT & OLIVES

The four basic flavors are sweet, sour, salt, and bitter. In the apricot-olive mixture, you get a symphony of these that can be paired with almost any protein. **makes 4 servings**

ingredients

2   8.8-ounce packages Uncle Ben's® Original Long-Grain White Ready Rice®
    Salt and freshly ground pepper
1   cup mixed Mediterranean olives in oil, drained, oil reserved
1¼ pounds beef tenderloin, cut into 1-inch cubes
1½ teaspoons Amore® garlic paste, or 2 garlic cloves, chopped
3   tablespoons sherry vinegar
1   cup apricot preserves
1   6-ounce package fresh baby spinach
⅓   cup chopped fresh flat-leaf parsley

method

1. Empty rice into a large microwave-safe bowl. Season with salt and pepper. Cover tightly with plastic wrap and microwave until rice is hot, about 5 minutes.
2. Meanwhile, heat 2 tablespoons of the reserved olive oil in a large sauté pan over high heat. Season beef with salt and pepper. Add to the pan and cook, stirring occasionally, until meat is evenly brown and medium-rare, about 6 minutes. Remove meat from pan. Cover lightly with foil to keep warm.
3. Add garlic to the pan and cook, stirring constantly, until fragrant, about 1½ minutes. Add sherry vinegar and stir, scraping the bottom of the pan to loosen any brown bits. Stir in apricot preserves. Bring mixture to a simmer and reduce to a sauce consistency, about 4 minutes. Stir in drained olives, beef, and spinach. Season to taste with salt and pepper, if necessary.
4. To serve, make a bed of the rice mixture on a platter. Spoon beef and sauce on top. Sprinkle with parsley.

grocery list

fresh

1¼ pounds beef tenderloin

1 bunch flat-leaf parsley

packaged

Two 8.8-ounce packages Uncle Ben's® Original Long-Grain White Ready Rice®

6-ounce package fresh baby spinach

12-ounce jar mixed Mediterranean olives in oil

3.15-ounce tube Amore® garlic paste

12-ounce jar apricot preserves

staples

sherry vinegar

tools

large sauté pan

QUICK FRICASSEE OF **BEEF** WITH BELGIAN ENDIVE & GRAPE TOMATOES

Belgian endive is great raw or cooked. When cooked, its natural bitterness—pleasant when raw—is intensified. The sweetness of the jelly plays an important role in mellowing it. **makes 4 servings**

grocery list

fresh
1½ pounds shell steak
4 heads Belgian endive
1 pint grape tomatoes

packaged
8-ounce jar thyme jelly

staples
vegetable oil
low-sodium chicken broth
Dijon mustard
butter

tools

large sauté pan

ingredients

2 tablespoons vegetable oil
1½ pounds shell steak, cut into bite-size pieces
Salt and freshly ground pepper
4 heads Belgian endive, sliced thinly crosswise
1 pint grape tomatoes
½ cup low-sodium chicken broth
¼ cup thyme or mint jelly
¼ cup Dijon mustard
2 tablespoons butter

method

1. Heat oil in a large sauté pan over high heat. Season beef with salt and pepper and add to the pan. Cook, stirring occasionally, until all sides are brown, about 3 minutes. Remove from pan.

2. Add endive to the pan and sauté, stirring occasionally, until it begins to wilt, about 3 minutes. Season to taste with salt and pepper. Add the tomatoes and chicken broth. Bring mixture to a simmer. Stir in the jelly (if you're using mint jelly, heat it for 20 to 30 seconds in the microwave before adding it to the pan), mustard, and butter. When butter has melted, return beef to the pan. Season to taste with salt and pepper, if necessary, and serve.

STIR-FRY OF **BEEF** WITH BLACK BEANS, RED PEPPERS & BROCCOLI

A little bit of last-minute, gently scrambled egg gives this chunky, textured stir fry a light, creamy element—and a smattering of bright yellow color. **makes 4 servings**

ingredients

2   tablespoons vegetable oil
1½ pounds sirloin, cut into bite-
      size pieces
      Salt and freshly ground
      pepper
1   11-ounce package frozen
      Pictsweet® Steamers
      Broccoli Florets with Red
      Peppers
1   15-ounce can black beans,
      rinsed and drained
1   8-ounce jar hoisin sauce
¾   cup low-sodium chicken
      broth
2   eggs

method

1. Heat oil in a large sauté pan over high heat. Season meat with salt and pepper; add to the pan. Cook, stirring occasionally, until all sides are brown, about 3 minutes. Remove beef from pan; set aside. Cover lightly with foil to keep warm.
2. Add frozen broccoli and peppers to the pan. Season with salt and pepper and sauté until defrosted, about 2 minutes. Add beans, hoisin sauce, and chicken broth to the pan; bring to a boil.
3. Break eggs into a bowl. Gently stir them into the pan to distribute throughout the sauce in streaks. Turn off the heat and allow eggs to coagulate, about 1 minute. (Do not mix at this point, or eggs will be broken into very small pieces.) Return beef to the pan and stir in very gently. Season to taste with salt and pepper, if necessary.

grocery list

fresh

1½ pounds sirloin

packaged

11-ounce package frozen Pictsweet® Steamers Broccoli Florets with Red Peppers

15-ounce can black beans

8-ounce jar hoisin sauce

staples

vegetable oil

low-sodium chicken broth

eggs

tools

large sauté pan

SWEET & SOUR CHERRY **BEEF** WITH ASPARAGUS & RED ONIONS

When considering the ingredients to add to a dish, I always look for compound flavors like preserves or chutneys. The cherry preserves make this dish look and taste like it took much more work to make than it actually did. **makes 4 servings**

grocery list

fresh

1½ pounds filet mignon

2 bunches asparagus

packaged

12-ounce jar sour cherry preserves

1-ounce package fresh tarragon

staples

vegetable oil

butter

red onion

red wine vinegar

tools

large cast-iron skillet

ingredients

2   tablespoons vegetable oil
1½ pounds filet mignon, cut into four 6-ounce portions, about 1 inch thick
       Salt and freshly ground pepper
4   tablespoons butter
2   bunches asparagus, cut on a bias into 1-inch pieces
1   large red onion, sliced thin
5   tablespoons red wine vinegar
¾   cup sour cherry preserves
3   tablespoons chopped fresh tarragon
1   tablespoon coarsely ground fresh black pepper

method

1. Heat oil in a large cast-iron skillet over high heat. When pan is hot, pat steaks dry with a paper towel and season generously with salt and pepper. Add steaks and cook 2 to 3 minutes per side for medium rare. Remove from pan. Cover with foil to keep warm.
2. Add butter to the pan and cook until butter is a deep golden-brown color. Add asparagus and onions and cook, stirring or tossing often, until the vegetables are tender and slightly browned, about 10 minutes. Season to taste with salt and pepper.
3. Add the red wine vinegar to the pan and allow to reduce by half, 2 to 3 minutes. Add the cherry preserves and cook until mixture has a sauce consistency, about 2 more minutes. Add the tarragon and the 1 tablespoon coarsely ground black pepper to the sauce. Season to taste with salt and pepper, if necessary.
4. Spoon sauce on a plate. Place a filet on top of sauce. Spoon asparagus-onion mixture on top of steak.

the fix

Great taste is all about balance of flavors. If you have too much sweet or too much sour in a dish, add more of the opposite flavor to compensate—sort of like mixing the amounts of blue and yellow paint to make a green that you like. In this recipe, the vinegar provides the sour, and the preserves, the sweet.

WARM ROAST **BEEF** & ENDIVE SALAD WITH PEPPERS & GREEK YOGURT

I love warm salads. They satisfy all kinds of cravings—for something warm and soul-soothing, as well for something loaded with crunchy, healthy vegetables. **makes 4 servings**

grocery list

fresh

4 heads Belgian endive

1 pound sliced roast beef

packaged

10-ounce jar Mancini® fried peppers

17.6-ounce container Fage® Total Greek yogurt

7-ounce bottle fish sauce

9-ounce jar Kikkoman® Thai-Style chili sauce

1 bunch fresh basil

staples

limes

tools

large sauté pan

ingredients

1 cup Mancini® fried peppers

4 heads Belgian endive, sliced crosswise about ½ inch thick

Salt and freshly ground pepper

1 cup Greek yogurt, preferably Fage®

3 tablespoons fish sauce

2 tablespoons Kikkoman® Thai-Style chili sauce

Juice of 2 limes

1 pound sliced roast beef, cut into 1-inch-wide strips

½ cup chopped fresh basil

method

1. Heat a large sauté pan over high heat. When hot, add fried peppers to the pan and sauté for about 1 minute. Next, add endive and season with salt and pepper. Cook until endive is slightly warm and slightly wilted, about 3 more minutes.

2. Meanwhile, make the dressing: In a large bowl, whisk together the yogurt, fish sauce, chili sauce, and lime juice. Add the endive mixture and the roast beef directly to the bowl of dressing along with the basil. Toss to coat evenly. Season to taste with salt and pepper, if necessary.

WARM ROAST **BEEF** & PROVOLONE SALAD WITH ARUGULA

Look for provolone that has been aged for about 12 months for this recipe—it has a firmer texture and tangier, more piquant flavor than the sweeter, milder provolone (also called dolce) that's only been aged for about 2 months. **makes 4 servings**

ingredients

1   pound sliced rare roast beef, cut into 1-inch squares
6   ounces sharp provolone cheese, cubed
2   cups grape tomatoes
3   tablespoons capers, drained
½   cup chopped fresh basil
1   6-ounce package baby arugula
1½ cups salad croutons
⅔   cup Marie's® Parmesan Ranch dressing
    Salt and freshly ground pepper

method

1. Preheat the oven to 300°F. Lay roast beef out on a rimmed baking sheet and place in the oven to warm. After about 3 minutes, add cheese cubes to the pan. Put pan back in oven. Bake for another 1 to 2 minutes, or until cheese is warm and starting to soften, but not melted.

2. In a large bowl, mix together the warmed roast beef and cheese with the tomatoes, capers, basil, arugula, croutons, and dressing. Season to taste with salt and pepper. Serve immediately.

grocery list

fresh

1 pound sliced rare roast beef

1 pint grape tomatoes

packaged

6-ounce package sharp provolone cheese

1-ounce package fresh basil

6-ounce package baby arugula

6-ounce box salad croutons

12-ounce jar Marie's® Parmesan Ranch dressing

staples

capers

tools

rimmed baking sheet

VIETNAMESE **BEEF** SALAD

Vietnamese cooks manage to pull together bright, vibrant flavors while keeping the dish light—and it's all thanks to the combination of fish sauce and fresh herbs. **makes 4 servings**

ingredients

4   tablespoons Kikkoman®
     Thai-Style Chili Sauce
1½ pounds filet mignon, cut into
     four 6-ounce portions,
     about 1 inch thick
     Salt and freshly ground
     pepper
1   large firm mango, peeled,
     pitted, and sliced thin
1   large seedless cucumber,
     peeled, halved horizontally,
     and thinly sliced into half
     moons
1   medium red onion, thinly
     sliced
½   cup Blue Dragon® Nuoc
     Cham dipping sauce
⅓   cup chopped fresh cilantro
⅓   cup chopped fresh mint

method

1. Preheat a grill/grill pan/broiler on high. Rub 2 tablespoons of the chili sauce into the meat. Season generously with salt and pepper. Grill meat about 3 minutes per side for medium rare. Remove from the grill and allow to rest and cool slightly, about 5 minutes.

2. Meanwhile, in a large bowl toss the remaining 2 tablespoons chili sauce with mango, cucumber, onion, dipping sauce, cilantro, and mint.

3. Slice beef thinly and toss gently with mango-cucumber mixture. Season to taste with salt and pepper and serve.

grocery list

fresh

1½ pounds filet mignon

1 large mango

1 large seedless cucumber

1 bunch cilantro

packaged

9-ounce jar Kikkoman®
Thai-Style Chili Sauce

8.45-ounce bottle Blue
Dragon® Nuoc Cham
dipping sauce

1 bunch fresh mint

staples

red onion

tools

grill pan

"

CHICKEN is incredibly versatile. It lends itself to all kinds of methods— from quick- cooking a cutlet to slow-roasting a whole bird.

"

ROASTED BUTTERFLIED **CHICKEN** WITH SHREDDED POTATOES, ONIONS & THYME

Maggie Silvestri and her husband were high school sweethearts. He totally spoils her and does all of the cooking. She knew he loved roast chicken, so she wanted to tackle it. **makes 4 servings**

ingredients

2   medium Idaho potatoes (about 1½ pounds total), peeled
1   4-pound boneless butterflied chicken (except for leg and wing bones) (see how-to photos, below)
    Salt and freshly ground pepper
3   tablespoons fresh thyme leaves
2   tablespoons Bertolli® extra-virgin olive oil
1   medium to large Vidalia onion, sliced very thin

method

1. Preheat oven to 400°F. Shred potatoes on a box grater. In two batches, wrap shredded potatoes in a clean kitchen towel. Hold over the sink and squeeze as much water out of potatoes as you can.
2. Heat a 14- to 16-inch cast-iron skillet over medium-high heat. Pat chicken dry; season with salt and pepper. Sprinkle skin side with 1 tablespoon of the thyme.
3. Add oil to the pan and carefully place chicken in pan skin side down. While chicken is browning, toss the potatoes with the onions and remaining 2 tablespoons of thyme leaves in a medium bowl. Season the mixture generously

with salt and pepper.
4. When chicken is browned, (after about 7 minutes), spread potatoes and onions evenly over chicken and place pan in oven.
5. After about 30 minutes of roasting, remove the pan from the oven and carefully turn the chicken out onto a large platter. Slide the chicken, potato-side down, back into the pan, along with any juices that may have accumulated on the platter.
6. Continue roasting until chicken is cooked through and edges of the potatoes are deeply browned and caramelized, 20 to 30 minutes. Serve in the skillet.

---

1. Place chicken, breast side down, on a cutting board. Use a serrated knife to make a cut down both sides of the backbone. Use a knife or kitchen shears to remove the wing tips. Discard backbone and wingtips.
2. Use a sharp knife to cut through the breastbone. This makes it easier for the chicken to lie flat, shortening the cooking time and making the bird easy to carve.

1.

2.

the fix

I had Maggie try her hand at butterflying the chicken. It took her 40 minutes, but she was such a good sport—and she did a great job. She forgot to brown the chicken and she burned the potatoes, so I tossed the singed potato cake, made a new one, browned the chicken, and reassembled the dish. No one was the wiser.

BOURSIN® & HAM-STUFFED **CHICKEN** WITH COUSCOUS & LENTIL SAUCE

Boursin®—essentially a flavored fresh French cheese—is awesome. It perfoms miracles in the kitchen. It's great for stuffing or for adding richness and flavor to a quick cream sauce. **makes 4 servings**

grocery list

fresh

4 chicken cutlets (about 1¼ pounds)

4 slices cooked ham

packaged

5.2-ounce package Black Pepper Boursin® cheese

3.15-ounce tube Amore® garlic paste

12-ounce package couscous

19-ounce can Progresso® Lentil Soup

staples

extra-virgin olive oil

tools

rimmed baking sheet

medium saucepan

ingredients

4   chicken cutlets, pounded thin, about 1¼ pounds
4   slices cooked ham
1   5.2-ounce package Black Pepper Boursin® cheese
2   tablespoons Bertolli® extra-virgin olive oil
2   tablespoons Amore® garlic paste, or 6 cloves garlic, chopped
     Salt and freshly ground pepper
2   cups water
1½   cups couscous
1   19-ounce can Progresso® Lentil Soup

method

1. Preheat broiler on high. Line a rimmed baking sheet with foil. Lay chicken cutlets on a work surface. Place one slice of ham on top of each cutlet. Cut Boursin® into quarters and place one piece in the center of each piece of ham. Fold cutlets over cheese and secure with a toothpick.

2. Mix together the olive oil and garlic paste and coat chicken with mixture. Season with salt and pepper and place on baking sheet. Broil until chicken is golden brown and cooked through and cheese is just starting to ooze, 4 to 5 minutes per side.

3. Meanwhile, bring water to boiling in a medium saucepan. Turn off the heat and stir in the couscous. Cover and let sit for 5 minutes; fluff with a fork.

4. In a medium microwaveable bowl, heat soup, covered, on high until simmering, about 4 minutes.

5. To serve, make a bed of couscous on a serving platter. Place stuffed chicken on top of couscous. Spoon lentil soup over top of the chicken.

BROILED **CHICKEN** THIGHS WITH BABA GHANOUSH, APRICOTS & CINNAMON

Eggplant sweetens, softens, and takes on a wonderful smoky flavor when it's broiled, as it is in garlicky baba ghanoush. Good news: The prepared stuff is widely available now. **makes 4 servings**

ingredients

2   pounds chicken thighs
    Salt and freshly ground
    pepper
2   teaspoons ground cinnamon
2   tablespoons Bertolli® extra-
    virgin olive oil
2   medium tomatoes, cut into
    large dice
2   7-ounce containers Sabra®
    baba ghanoush
1   cup dried apricots, roughly
    chopped
½   cup chopped fresh mint

method

1. Preheat broiler on high. Season thighs generously with salt and pepper and cinnamon. Place thighs, skin sides down, on a roasting rack set on a rimmed, foil-lined baking sheet. Broil for about 10 minutes. Turn and continue to broil until skin is deep golden brown and chicken is just cooked through, another 5 to 6 minutes.
2. Meanwhile, heat olive oil in a large sauté pan over medium heat. Add tomatoes and season with salt and pepper. Cook, stirring, for about 1 minute. Add baba ghanoush and apricots. Continue to cook, stirring occasionally, until mixture is hot throughout, 3 to 4 minutes. Season to taste with salt and pepper; stir in mint. Serve with chicken.

grocery list

fresh

2 pounds chicken thighs

2 medium tomatoes

packaged

Two 7-ounce containers
Sabra® baba ghanoush

6-ounce package
dried apricots

1 bunch fresh mint

staples

ground cinnamon

extra-virgin olive oil

tools

rimmed baking sheet

large sauté pan

BROILED **CHICKEN** THIGHS WITH STEW OF MUSHROOMS, CORN & CABBAGE

Cremini mushrooms are abundantly available and slightly more flavorful than white mushrooms—and don't stain your food like the juice of the ubiquitous portobello. **makes 4 servings**

grocery list

fresh
2 pounds chicken thighs
1 bunch scallions

packaged
3.15-ounce tube Amore® garlic paste
8-ounce package sliced cremini mushrooms
16-ounce package coleslaw mix
10-ounce package frozen corn
12.5-ounce jar House of Tsang® General Tso's Sauce

staples
vegetable oil

tools

rimmed baking sheet

large sauté pan

ingredients

5 tablespoons vegetable oil
3 tablespoons Amore® garlic paste, or 9 garlic cloves, chopped
2 pounds chicken thighs
Salt and freshly ground pepper
1 8-ounce package sliced cremini mushrooms
1 bunch scallions, sliced thin on a bias (see how-to photos, page 21)
1 16-ounce package coleslaw mix
1½ cups frozen corn kernels
1 12.5-ounce jar House of Tsang® General Tso's Sauce
¼ cup water

method

1. Combine 2 tablespoons of the vegetable oil with the garlic paste. Rub the mixture over the chicken thighs to coat. (If desired, put thighs in a resealable plastic bag in the refrigerator and marinate overnight.)

2. Preheat broiler on high. Season chicken generously with salt and pepper. Place, skin side down, on a roasting rack set on a foil-lined, rimmed baking sheet. Broil for about 10 minutes. Turn and continue to broil until skin is deep golden brown and chicken is just cooked through, 5 to 6 minutes more.

3. Meanwhile, heat remaining 3 tablespoons oil over high heat in a large sauté pan. When oil is hot, add mushrooms and cook, stirring occasionally, until golden brown, about 6 minutes. Stir in scallions, coleslaw mix, and corn, and season to taste with salt and pepper. Cover and cook until cabbage is tender, about 4 minutes.

4. Add General Tso's Sauce and water to the vegetable mixture. Season to taste with salt and pepper, if necessary. Serve vegetable mixture with chicken thighs.

COCONUT-GINGER **CHICKEN** STIR-FRY WITH BROCCOLI & RICE

Coco Lopez—the rich, creamy stuff that is the central ingredient in the piña colada—is a guilty pleasure of mine. It's not really that good for you (OK, that's an understatement), but it sure does taste good. Look for it in the liquor aisle of your supermarket or at the liquor store. **makes 4 servings**

ingredients

2   8.8-ounce packages Uncle Ben's® Long Grain White Ready Rice®
3   tablespoons toasted sesame oil
1¼ pounds chicken stir-fry meat
    Salt and freshly ground pepper
1   head broccoli, cut into bite-size pieces
1   cup Coco Lopez®
¼   teaspoon cayenne pepper
¼   cup high-quality soy sauce
¼   cup chopped pickled ginger (sushi ginger, also called gari)

method

1. Heat the rice in the pouch, according to package directions.

2. Meanwhile, heat 2 tablespoons of the sesame oil in a large cast-iron skillet over high heat. Season chicken generously with salt and pepper and add to the pan. Cook, stirring occasionally, until chicken is golden brown and just cooked through, about 5 minutes. Remove chicken from pan; cover lightly with foil to keep warm.

3. Add remaining tablespoon of sesame oil to the pan and add broccoli. Stir-fry until broccoli is lightly cooked but still crisp, about 2 minutes. Add Coco Lopez and cayenne to the pan and bring to a simmer. Cook, stirring occasionally, until sauce thickens and broccoli is tender, 3 to 4 minutes.

4. Add soy sauce, pickled ginger, and chicken to the pan and stir to combine. Season to taste with salt and pepper, if necessary. Serve chicken mixture over a bed of rice.

grocery list

fresh

1¼ pounds chicken for stir fry

1 head broccoli

packaged

Two 8.8-ounce packages Uncle Ben's® Long Grain White Ready Rice®

12-ounce can Coco Lopez®

4-ounce container pickled ginger

staples

toasted sesame oil

cayenne pepper

soy sauce

tools

large cast-iron skillet

BROILED **CHICKEN** LEGS WITH ONIONS, APPLES & CHUNKY LEMON-PEPPER SAUCE

Chicken legs are my desert-island food. Never been a breast man—they can be dry and flavorless—but gimme a juicy leg any day of the week. **makes 4 servings**

ingredients

2½ pounds chicken legs
   Salt and freshly ground pepper
2 large Vidalia onions, peeled
2 Granny Smith apples, peeled, cored, and quartered
2 tablespoons Bertolli® extra-virgin olive oil
1 10-ounce jar Tabasco® Spicy Red Pepper Jelly
3 lemons
   Fresh coarsely ground black pepper

method

1. Preheat broiler on low. Line a rimmed baking sheet with foil. Season chicken generously with salt and pepper. Place chicken in center of pan.
2. Cut each onion into 12 thin wedges. Scatter onions and apples around chicken. Drizzle everything with olive oil and season with salt and pepper. Broil for 10 minutes. Turn chicken over and stir apples and onions to expose uncooked surfaces. Turn broiler on high. Broil until chicken is charred and cooked through, about another 10 minutes.
3. Meanwhile, heat pepper jelly in a small saucepan until melted. Peel the lemons and remove the pith. Dice the lemons, reserving the juice. Remove jelly from heat; add diced lemon and juice. Stir to combine and season to taste with salt and pepper.
4. To serve, spoon sauce on top of chicken, onions, and apples and top with fresh coarsely ground pepper.

grocery list

fresh
2½ pounds chicken legs
2 Granny Smith apples

packaged
10-ounce jar Tabasco® Spicy Red Pepper Jelly

staples
Vidalia onions
extra-virgin olive oil
lemons

tools

rimmed baking sheet

small saucepan

CREAMY **CHICKEN** WITH PESTO & TOMATO WRAPPED IN TOASTED FLATBREAD

The "creamy" part of this dish comes in the form of a pesto mayo. Char the flatbread a little—biting through the crusty bread into the creamy filling is a yummy experience. **makes 4 servings**

grocery list

fresh

One 1½-pound rotisserie chicken

1 pint grape tomatoes

packaged

7.5-ounce jar Paesana™ pesto sauce

14-ounce package 8-inch flatbreads

5-ounce package baby arugula

staples

extra-virgin olive oil

light mayonnaise

Parmigiano-Reggiano cheese

tools

large sauté pan

rimmed baking sheet

ingredients

2 tablespoons Bertolli® extra-virgin olive oil
1 pint grape tomatoes
   Salt and freshly ground pepper
1 cup light mayonnaise
¼ cup Paesana™ pesto sauce
1 1½ pound rotisserie chicken, meat removed and shredded (see how-to photos, page 78)
⅔ cup grated Parmigiano-Reggiano cheese
4 8-inch flatbreads
1 5-ounce package baby arugula

method

1. Heat 1 tablespoon of the olive oil in a large sauté pan over medium-high heat. Add the tomatoes; season to taste with salt and pepper. Cover and cook until tomatoes release their juice and are wilted and soft, about 5 minutes. Meanwhile, in a large bowl mix together the mayonnaise and pesto; toss with chicken. Add chicken mixture to the pan with tomatoes and cook, stirring occasionally, just until chicken is very warm. Stir in cheese; season to taste with salt and pepper.
2. Preheat broiler on low. Line a rimmed baking sheet with foil. Divide chicken mixture among the flatbreads. Fold flatbreads in half and secure with a toothpick. Place flatbreads on baking sheet and broil until deep golden brown, about 1 minute per side. (Keep a close eye on them while broiling, as they brown quickly.)
3. In a medium bowl, toss arugula with remaining tablespoon of olive oil; season to taste with salt and pepper. Remove toothpicks from flatbreads and serve with salad.

the fix
If you burn your flatbread under the broiler—and admittedly, it's easy to do—just scrape the filling out and replace it. (And don't walk away from the stove.) Incineration of the bread does no harm to the filling.

HONEY-MUSTARD **CHICKEN** WITH FRESH GARLIC BREAD & BROCCOLI RABE

I started to sauté bread to make croutons when I was in cooking school because I used to burn them too often in the oven. I prefer that method to this day. **makes 4 servings**

ingredients

5   tablespoons Bertolli® extra-virgin olive oil
2   tablespoons Amore® garlic paste, or 6 garlic cloves, chopped
½   baguette, torn into bite-size chunks, about 6 cups
    Salt and freshly ground pepper
1   head broccoli rabe, cut into bite-size pieces
1   teaspoon crushed red pepper
¾   cup dry white wine
1   8-ounce jar honey mustard, preferably Maille® honey Dijon
1   1½-pound rotisserie chicken, meat removed and shredded (see how-to photos, page 78)

method

1. Heat 4 tablespoons of the olive oil over medium heat in a large sauté pan. When oil is hot, add garlic paste, stirring to break it up. Add bread chunks to the pan, stirring to coat. Cook bread, stirring occasionally, until golden brown but still soft on the interior, 3 to 4 minutes. Season generously with salt and pepper. Remove from the pan and drain on a paper towel-lined plate.

2. Add remaining tablespoon oil to the pan. When hot, add broccoli rabe. Cover and cook, stirring occasionally, until tender, about 4 minutes. Season to taste with salt and pepper. Add red pepper, wine, and mustard; bring to a simmer. Add chicken, stirring to combine. Continue to cook until chicken is hot, 3 to 4 minutes. To serve, spoon chicken on top of bread.

grocery list

fresh

1 baguette

1 head broccoli rabe

One 1½-pound rotisserie chicken

packaged

3.15-ounce tube Amore® garlic paste

8-ounce jar Maille® honey Dijon

staples

extra-virgin olive oil

crushed red pepper

dry white wine

tools

large sauté pan

TURKEY STEAKS WITH SWEET POTATO, ROASTED ALMONDS & POMEGRANATE VINAIGRETTE

Sweet potatoes and pomegranate is a flavor combination I've been loving for years now—the sweet with the tart is great together. **makes 4 servings**

grocery list

fresh

4 turkey or chicken cutlets (about 1¼ pounds)

packaged

16-ounce bottle POM Wonderful® pomegranate juice

2-pound package Diner's Choice® mashed sweet potatoes

⅔-ounce package fresh tarragon

2.25-ounce package sliced almonds

staples

extra-virgin olive oil

sliced almonds

tools

large sauté pan

grill pan

ingredients

2 cups POM Wonderful® pomegranate juice

4 turkey or chicken cutlets, about 1¼ pounds

¼ cup plus 2 tablespoons Bertolli® extra-virgin olive oil

Salt and freshly ground pepper

1 2-pound package Diner's Choice® mashed sweet potatoes

¼ cup chopped tarragon

½ cup sliced almonds, toasted

method

1. In a large sauté pan bring pomegranate juice to a full boil. Cook until reduced to ½ cup, about 7 minutes.

2. Preheat grill/grill pan/broiler on high. Coat turkey with the 2 tablespoons olive oil and season generously with salt and pepper. Grill until just cooked through, about 2 to 3 minutes per side.

3. Meanwhile, heat sweet potatoes according to package directions. Combine pomegranate reduction with tarragon and the ¼ cup olive oil; season to taste with salt and pepper.

4. To serve, make a bed of sweet potatoes on a platter. Top with grilled turkey (sliced, if desired). Spoon pomegranate vinaigrette over the turkey and sprinkle almonds on top.

ROTISSERIE **CHICKEN** & WARM BULGUR SALAD WITH YOGURT-PARSLEY DRESSING

To squeeze the maximum amount of juice from lemons, roll them on the counter before you juice them. It separates the flesh from the skin, making them release more juice. **makes 4 servings**

grocery list

fresh

large tomato

1 bunch flat-leaf parsley

One 1½-pound rotisserie chicken

packaged

28-ounce package Bob's Red Mill® bulgur

17.6-ounce container Fage® Total Greek yogurt

staples

red onion

lemons

tools

large saucepan

ingredients

1½ cups water
1½ cups Bob's Red Mill® bulgur
    Salt and freshly ground pepper
1   large tomato, cut into large dice
1   small red onion, cut into small dice
1   bunch chopped fresh flat-leaf parsley
    Juice and zest of 3 lemons
1   cup Greek yogurt, preferably Fage®
1   1½-pound warm rotisserie chicken, meat removed and torn into bite-size chunks (see how-to photos, page 78)

method

1. In a large saucepan bring water and bulgur to a boil. Season with salt and pepper; cover and turn off heat. Allow to sit until water is absorbed and bulgur is tender, 25 to 30 minutes.
2. In a large bowl, combine the warm bulgur, tomato, red onion, all but ½ cup of the parsley, and the juice and zest of 2 lemons. Season generously with salt and pepper.
3. In a medium bowl, combine the yogurt with the juice and zest of the remaining lemon and the reserved ½ cup parsley. Add chicken to the bowl and toss to combine. Season to taste with salt and pepper. Serve chicken on a bed of the warm bulgur salad.

the fix
If—even after sitting for 25 or 30 minutes—the bulgur hasn't softened enough, just pour a little boiling water or stock over it. This will work even if you've already added the tomatoes, onion, parsley, and lemon juice and zest to it. Let it sit a few minutes more, until it's pleasantly chewy, then proceed with the recipe.

WARM **CHICKEN** SALAD WITH TAHINI-YOGURT DRESSING & WATERCRESS

Tahini is a sesame seed paste that's used as a condiment in many Middle Eastern dishes. It has a rich, toasty, bold flavor that blends well with tart, creamy yogurt. **makes 4 servings**

ingredients

½   cup apricot jam
1   cup Paesana™ Fire-Roasted Peppers with Garlic and Extra Virgin Olive Oil
1   1½-pound rotisserie chicken, meat removed and shredded (see how-to photos, page 78)
½   cup Greek yogurt, preferably Fage®
½   cup tahini, preferably Sabra® Juice and zest of 2 lemons Salt and freshly ground pepper
1   6-ounce package watercress
¾   cup chopped fresh mint

method

1. In a large sauté pan over medium-high heat, melt apricot jam. Add red peppers; stir until warmed through. Add chicken and cook, stirring often, until chicken is hot.

2. Meanwhile, mix together yogurt, tahini, and the juice and zest of the lemons. Stir into chicken and peppers. Season to taste with salt and pepper.

3. In a large bowl toss chicken mixture with watercress and mint. Season to taste with salt and black pepper, if necessary.

grocery list

fresh

One 1½-pound rotisserie chicken

packaged

12-ounce jar apricot jam

12-ounce jar Paesana™ Fire-Roasted Peppers with Garlic and Extra Virgin Olive Oil

7-ounce container Fage® Total Greek yogurt

7-ounce container Sabra® tahini

6-ounce package watercress

1 bunch fresh mint

staples

lemons

tools

large sauté pan

CHICKEN & CHORIZO STEW WITH
MUSTARD GREENS & CORN

Chorizo is a spicy Spanish pork sausage that perfumes whatever it touches with the unique blend of spices—including chili, paprika, and garlic—that makes a chorizo a chorizo. **makes 4 servings**

grocery list

fresh

6-ounce link chorizo
1 bunch mustard greens
One 1½-pound rotisserie chicken

packaged

3.15-ounce tube Amore® garlic paste

10-ounce package frozen corn

staples

extra-virgin olive oil
crushed red pepper
low-sodium chicken broth

tools

large sauté pan

ingredients

2   tablespoons Bertolli® extra-virgin olive oil
1   6-ounce link chorizo, cut into a small dice (see how-to photos, page 65)
3   tablespoons Amore® garlic paste, or 9 cloves garlic, chopped
5   cups cleaned, chopped mustard greens
    Salt and freshly ground pepper
1   teaspoon crushed red pepper
2   14.5-ounce cans low-sodium chicken broth
1   cup frozen corn kernels
1   1½-pound warm rotisserie chicken, meat removed and torn into bite-size chunks (see how-to photos, page 79)

method

1. Heat olive oil in a large sauté pan over medium heat. When oil is hot, add chorizo and cook until fat starts to render, about 2 minutes.
2. Stir in garlic paste and cook, stirring, for about 1 more minute. Turn heat up to high and add mustard greens; season to taste with salt and pepper. Cover and cook until greens are wilted and tender, about 4 minutes.
3. Add red pepper, chicken broth, and corn. Bring to a simmer. Add chicken. Season to taste with salt and pepper and serve.

the fix

Chorizo can vary pretty widely in how it's seasoned. If you find you've bought chorizo that is just too spicy, add a little butter to the dish right before serving—it helps to mellow the heat.

1. Start by setting the chorizo link on a cutting board. Using a sharp knife, cut the chorizo link in half lengthwise.

2. If desired, for smaller pieces, cut each chorizo half in half lengthwise again. Lay chorizo quarters side by side (flat sides down).

3. Hold the link pieces with one hand, curling your fingertips under so they don't get in the way of the knife. Cut the chorizo into slices.

4. Continue to slice the chorizo pieces, moving your hand down as you cut.

5. When you're finished slicing the chorizo, carefully use your knife blade and your other hand to scoop up the chunks of chorizo. Place the chorizo on a small plate or bowl and set aside until ready to use.

SAFFRON-SCENTED **CHICKEN** STEW WITH BACON & ARTICHOKES

Saffron is the stigma of the crocus sativa flower. It's harvested by hand—which explains the price. But it has a dreamy scent and flavor that's worth the indulgence once in a while. **makes 4 servings**

grocery list

fresh

½ pound bacon

One 1½-pound rotisserie chicken

packaged

Two 8.8-ounce packages Uncle Ben's® Vegetable Harvest Ready Whole Grain Medley™

3.15-ounce tube Amore® garlic paste

14-ounce can quartered artichoke hearts

staples

low-sodium chicken broth

saffron

sour cream

tools

Dutch oven

ingredients

2 8.8-ounce packages Uncle Ben's® Vegetable Harvest Ready Whole Grain Medley™

½ pound bacon, cut into thin strips

2 tablespoons Amore® garlic paste, or 6 garlic cloves, chopped

1 14.5-ounce can low-sodium chicken broth

½ teaspoon saffron

1 14-ounce can quartered artichoke hearts, drained

1 1½-pound warm rotisserie chicken, meat removed and torn into bite-size chunks (see how-to photos, page 78)

½ cup sour cream
   Salt and freshly ground pepper

method

1. Heat rice in pouch according to package directions.

2. Meanwhile, heat a Dutch oven over medium-high heat. Add bacon and cook, stirring often, until bacon begins to brown but is not crisp, about 4 minutes. Stir in garlic paste and cook, stirring, for 1 minute more. Add chicken broth and saffron and bring to a simmer.

3. Turn heat down to low and stir in artichoke hearts. When artichoke hearts are hot, stir in chicken. Stir in sour cream; season to taste with salt and pepper.

4. Ladle stew over bowls of rice and serve.

SPICY SZECHUAN **TURKEY**, CARROT & RADICCHIO STIR FRY

If a dish has the word "Szechuan" in its name, it usually means it's spicy—because of the commonly used Szechuan pepper. It's not actually related to black pepper and isn't really hot itself, but rather contains a compound that sets the stage for chilies and other pungent ingredients. **makes 4 servings**

ingredients

2   8.8-ounce packages Uncle Ben's® Original Long-Grain White Ready Rice®
    Salt and freshly ground pepper
4   tablespoons toasted sesame oil
1½ pounds turkey or chicken breast, cut into bite-size chunks
1   10-ounce package shredded carrots
1   large head radicchio, shredded, about 4 cups
1   11.5-ounce bottle House of Tsang® Szechuan Spicy™ stir-fry sauce
⅔   cup chopped fresh cilantro

method

1. Empty rice into a medium microwaveable bowl. Season with salt and pepper, if necessary. Cover with plastic wrap and microwave on high until hot, 3 to 4 minutes.
2. Meanwhile, heat 2 tablespoons of the sesame oil over high heat in a large sauté pan or cast-iron skillet. Season turkey with salt and pepper; add to the pan. Stir-fry turkey until golden brown and just cooked through, about 6 minutes.
3. Remove turkey from the pan; cover lightly with foil to keep warm. Add remaining 2 tablespoons sesame oil to the pan. Add carrots and radicchio to the pan and stir-fry until wilted but not soft, about 3 minutes. Add sauce; bring to a simmer. Return turkey to the pan and stir in cilantro. Season to taste with salt and pepper, if necessary; serve over rice.

grocery list

fresh

1½ pounds turkey or chicken breast

1 large head radicchio

1 bunch cilantro

packaged

Two 8.8-ounce packages Uncle Ben's® Original Long-Grain White Ready Rice®

10-ounce package shredded carrots

11.5-ounce bottle House of Tsang® Szechuan Spicy™ stir fry sauce

staples

toasted sesame oil

tools

medium microwaveable bowl

large sauté pan

FRICASSEE OF BONELESS **CHICKEN** THIGHS, CARROTS, RAISINS & CUMIN

Chopping carrots in a hurry is an exercise in frustration. They roll around and don't easily cut uniformly. I use a lot of pre-cut carrots, like carrot slaw—or carrot-raisin salad. **makes 4 servings**

grocery list

fresh

1½ pounds boneless chicken thighs

1½ pounds store-bought carrot-raisin salad

packaged

15-ounce box Sun-Maid® Mixed Jumbo Raisins

Two 8-ounce containers Pacific® Natural Foods Cashew Carrot Ginger Soup

1-ounce package fresh basil

staples

cider vinegar

vegetable oil

ground cumin

tools

small microwaveable bowl

large cast-iron skillet

ingredients

1 cup Sun-Maid® Mixed Jumbo Raisins
⅓ cup cider vinegar
1 tablespoon vegetable oil
1½ pounds boneless chicken thighs
Salt and freshly ground pepper
1 teaspoon ground cumin
1½ pounds store-bought carrot-raisin salad
1¼ cups Pacific® Natural Foods Cashew Carrot Ginger Soup
¾ cup chopped basil

method

1. In a small microwaveable bowl combine raisins and vinegar. Cover with plastic wrap and microwave on high for 3 to 4 minutes, or until raisins have plumped up; set aside.

2. Meanwhile, in a large cast-iron skillet or sauté pan, heat oil over medium-high heat. Season chicken with salt and pepper; carefully place in pan, skin side down. When skin is golden brown, after about 7 minutes, turn thighs. Continue cooking until chicken is cooked through, about 4 more minutes. Remove chicken from pan; cover lightly with foil to keep warm.

3. Drain all but 2 tablespoons of fat from the pan. Add cumin and carrot salad and cook, stirring, until carrots are almost tender, about 3 minutes. Season to taste with salt and pepper. Add raisins, soup, and basil; bring to a simmer. Season to taste with salt and pepper, if necessary. Return chicken to pan and serve.

SALSA VERDE STIR-FRIED **CHICKEN** & VEGETABLES WITH BACON

Salsa verde literally means "green sauce," and every culture has its own version. Here I'm referring to a tomatillo-based salsa used in Mexican cooking. **makes 4 servings**

grocery list

fresh

1½ pounds chicken for stir-fry

½ pound thick-cut bacon

packaged

12-ounce package Mann's California Stir Fry® vegetables

16-ounce bottle mild salsa verde

staples

vegetable oil

honey

tools

large sauté pan

ingredients

2   tablespoons vegetable oil
1½ pounds stir-fry chicken
      Salt and freshly ground
      pepper
½   pound thick-cut bacon, cut
      into thin strips
1   12-ounce package Mann's
      California Stir Fry®
      vegetables
⅓   cup honey
2   cups mild salsa verde

method

1. In a large sauté pan heat vegetable oil over high heat. Season chicken generously with salt and pepper. Cook, stirring occasionally, until golden brown and just cooked through, about 5 minutes. Remove from pan; cover lightly with foil to keep warm.
2. Add bacon to the pan and cook, stirring often, until fat has rendered and bacon is beginning to turn golden brown. Add vegetables and stir-fry until they are tender, about 6 minutes. Add honey and salsa verde; bring to a simmer. Season vegetables to taste with salt and pepper. Return chicken to the pan. Stir to combine and serve.

SAUTÉED **CHICKEN** CUTLETS WITH SAUSAGE & PEPPERS

I love fried peppers, but cleaning, slicing, and frying your own takes some doing. Jarred fried peppers are fabulous. They taste great, and to be able to open a jar and skip five prep steps is a very good thing. **makes 4 servings**

ingredients

½ cup Bertolli® light olive oil
    Salt and freshly ground
      pepper
1 cup all-purpose flour
4 chicken cutlets, about
      1¼ pounds
2 eggs, lightly beaten
2 links hot Italian sausage,
      casing removed
⅔ cup dry red wine
2 10-ounce jars Mancini® fried
      peppers
1 24-ounce jar Bertolli®
      Vineyard Portobello
      Mushroom with Merlot
      pasta sauce

method

1. In a large sauté pan heat olive oil over high heat. Meanwhile, season chicken with salt and pepper. Put flour in a shallow plate; dredge cutlets in flour and then dip in egg. When oil is hot, add cutlets to the pan. Cook until golden brown and just cooked through, about 3 minutes per side. Remove cutlets from pan; cover lightly with foil to keep warm.

2. Wipe pan with a clean paper towel; add sausage. Cook until golden brown and cooked through, about 6 minutes. Add red wine; bring to a simmer. Add fried peppers and pasta sauce; return to a simmer. Season to taste with salt and pepper. To serve, lay chicken on a platter and pour sausage-pepper mixture on top.

grocery list

fresh

4 chicken cutlets (about
1¼ pounds)

2 links hot Italian sausage

packaged

Two 10-ounce jars
Mancini® fried peppers

24-ounce jar Bertolli®
Vineyard Portobello
Mushroom with Merlot
pasta pauce

staples

light olive oil

flour

eggs

dry red wine

tools

large sauté pan

GRILLED **TURKEY** STEAKS WITH SAUTÉED BELGIAN ENDIVE, BACON & MANGO CHUTNEY

Grilled turkey breast cutlets are the lightest, quickest, healthiest dish I can think of. Always buy "thin" cutlets to save yourself cooking time. **makes 4 servings**

grocery list

fresh

4 turkey or chicken cutlets (about 1¼ pounds)

½ pound thick-cut bacon

1 bunch scallions

4 large heads Belgian endive

packaged

9-ounce jar Crosse and Blackwell® hot mango chutney

staples

extra-virgin olive oil

tools

grill pan

large sauté pan

ingredients

4 turkey or chicken cutlets, pounded thin, about 1¼ pounds

2 tablespoons Bertolli® extra-virgin olive oil
Salt and freshly ground pepper

½ pound thick-cut bacon, cut into lardons (see how-to photos, page 73)

1 bunch scallions, sliced thin on a bias (see how-to photos, page 21)

4 large heads Belgian endive, sliced crosswise about ½ inch thick

1 9-ounce jar Crosse and Blackwell® hot mango chutney

method

1. Preheat grill/grill pan/broiler on high. Coat turkey with olive oil; season with salt and pepper. Grill until turkey is just cooked through, 2 to 3 minutes per side.

2. Meanwhile, cook bacon in a large sauté pan over medium heat. When bacon is golden brown, add scallions and endive to the pan; season to taste with salt and pepper. Cook, stirring occasionally, until endive is tender, about 4 minutes. Add chutney to the pan; stir to combine. Season to taste with salt and pepper, if necessary.

1. Remove the bacon from its packaging, keeping the slab in one piece. Set the bacon on a cutting board.

2. Using a sharp knife, and starting on one side, cut the bacon slab crosswise into very thin strips.

3. Continue cutting the bacon slab into strips, sliding your hand down the length of the slab as you go.

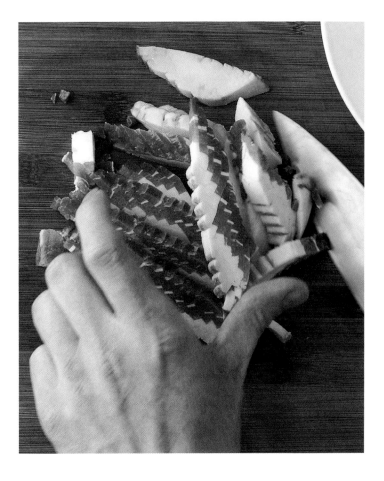

4. You only need ½ pound of bacon, so stop cutting strips about halfway through the 1-pound slab. Wrap the remaining bacon and refrigerate for another use.

5. Use one hand to scoop the lardons onto the flat edge of your knife. Place the lardons on a plate and set aside until ready to use.

GRILLED WASABI-GINGER **CHICKEN** KEBABS WITH MUSHROOMS & LIMA BEANS

I love lima beans. They freeze well and don't have the heavy texture some other beans have. They also have a mild sweetness to them—more like a pea than a bean. **makes 4 servings**

ingredients

2 tablespoons wasabi paste

2 cups prepared Asian-style ginger dressing

4 prepared chicken kebabs, about 1½ pounds

Salt and freshly ground pepper

2 tablespoons vegetable oil

1 12-ounce package mixed wild mushrooms

1 15-ounce can lima beans, rinsed and drained

½ cup chopped fresh cilantro

method

1. In a small bowl combine wasabi and ½ cup of the ginger dressing. Place kebabs in a resealable plastic bag and pour marinade over them. Seal the bag and marinate at room temperature for 15 minutes or in the refrigerator overnight.

2. Preheat grill/grill pan/broiler on high. Season kebabs generously with salt and pepper. Grill, rotating kebabs on all four sides, until chicken is charred and just cooked through, about 12 minutes.

3. Meanwhile, in a large sauté pan heat vegetable oil over medium-high heat. Add mushrooms to the pan and turn heat up to high. Cook, stirring frequently, until mushrooms are golden brown and tender, about 7 minutes. Season to taste with salt and pepper.

4. Add lima beans and remaining ginger dressing to the pan; bring to a simmer. Stir in the cilantro and season to taste with salt and pepper, if necessary. Serve kebabs with the mushroom mixture.

grocery list

fresh

4 prepared chicken kebabs (about 1½ pounds)

1 bunch cilantro

packaged

1.52-ounce tube wasabi paste

15-ounce bottle Asian-style ginger dressing

12-ounce package mixed wild mushrooms

15-ounce can lima beans

staples

vegetable oil

tools

grill pan

large sauté pan

STIR-FRY OF **CHICKEN** WITH HOT & SWEET PEANUT SAUCE & GREEN RICE

Indian and Mexican cooking have versions of green rice—white rice made colorful and flavorful with chiles, fresh herbs, or both. Here, a simple stir-in of lots of fresh mint does the trick. **makes 4 servings**

grocery list

fresh

1¼ pounds chicken for stir-fry

packaged

Two 8.8-ounce packages Uncle Ben's® Original Long-Grain White Ready Rice®

8-ounce package fresh sugar snap peas

Tiger Tiger™ Hoisin Sauce

1 bunch fresh mint

staples

vegetable oil

chunky peanut butter

Tabasco® sauce

tools

large sauté pan

ingredients

2   8.8-ounce packages Uncle Ben's® Original Long-Grain White Ready Rice®
3   tablespoons vegetable oil
1¼ pounds chicken for stir fry
    Salt and freshly ground pepper
1   8-ounce package fresh sugar snap peas
1   cup Tiger Tiger™ Hoisin Sauce
½   cup chunky peanut butter
⅔   cup water
3   tablespoons Tabasco® sauce
2   cups chopped fresh mint

method

1. Heat rice in pouches according to package directions.

2. Meanwhile, in a large sauté pan heat 2 tablespoons vegetable oil over high heat. Season chicken with salt and pepper; add to pan. Cook, stirring occasionally, until golden brown and cooked through, about 5 minutes. Remove chicken from pan; cover lightly with foil to keep warm.

3. Add remaining tablespoon of oil to pan. When oil is hot, add snap peas; cook, stirring occasionally, until almost tender, about 3 minutes.

4. In a medium bowl, whisk together hoisin sauce, peanut butter, water, and Tabasco until smooth. Add sauce mixture and chicken to pan; bring to a simmer. Season to taste with salt and pepper, if necessary.

5. In a medium bowl toss hot rice with mint. Season to taste with salt and pepper. Serve chicken mixture over rice.

SWEET & SOUR BAKED **CHICKEN** TENDERS WITH TREVISANO

Sweet and sour is a great go-to sauce—almost everyone seems to like it—and there are many, many good ones out there. **makes 4 servings**

ingredients

1¼ pounds chicken tenders
2 eggs, lightly beaten
2 cups finely crushed tortilla chips
 Salt and freshly ground pepper
2 tablespoons vegetable oil
4 heads trevisano, halved and sliced crosswise into ½-inch pieces, about 9 cups (or 4 heads radicchio, quartered and sliced in ½-inch pieces)
1 17-ounce jar MIKEE® Authentic Chinese Rib Sauce, or sweet and sour sauce of choice
⅔ cup chopped fresh basil

method

1. Preheat oven to 400°F. Dip chicken tenders in eggs, then coat in the crushed tortilla chips. Place on a foil-lined rimmed baking sheet. Season with salt and pepper; bake until golden brown and just cooked through, 10 to 12 minutes.

2. Meanwhile, in a large sauté pan heat vegetable oil over high heat. Add trevisano; season to taste with salt and pepper. Cook, tossing often, until wilted and tender, about 4 minutes. Stir in about two-thirds of the jar of rib sauce and basil. Season to taste with salt and pepper, if necessary. Gently toss chicken tenders with remaining sauce; serve on top of the trevisano mixture.

grocery list

fresh

1¼ pounds chicken tenders

4 heads trevisano

packaged

13-ounce package tortilla chips

17-ounce jar MIKEE® Authentic Chinese Rib Sauce

1-ounce package fresh basil

staples

eggs

vegetable oil

tools

rimmed baking sheet

large sauté pan

the assist

Trevisano is a kind of radicchio. Its heads are more oblong than round and the striped leaves looser than standard radicchio. It's almost floral in its appearance. It is truly a gorgeous vegetable, but if you can't find it, regular radicchio works just fine.

WARM **CHICKEN** & RADICCHIO SALAD WITH ORANGE, TARRAGON & GOAT CHEESE

Segment an orange by slicing the top and bottom off, then cutting the peel off down the sides. Then just cut toward the center of the orange on either side of each segment to release. **makes 4 servings**

grocery list

fresh

2 large heads radicchio

One 1½-pound rotisserie chicken

6-ounces goat cheese

packaged

1-ounce package fresh tarragon

staples

extra-virgin olive oil

sherry vinegar

oranges

bread

tools

large sauté pan

ingredients

¼ cup Bertolli® extra-virgin olive oil

2 large heads radicchio, shredded, about 7 cups
Salt and freshly ground pepper

3 tablespoons sherry vinegar

3 oranges, peeled and cut into segments, juice reserved

1 1½-pound warm rotisserie chicken, meat removed and shredded (see how-to photos, page 79)

6 ounces fresh goat cheese, broken into small chunks

¼ cup chopped fresh tarragon

1 cup toasted bread chunks or croutons

method

1. In a large sauté pan heat oil over high heat. Add radicchio and season generously with salt and pepper. Cook, stirring, until warm and just slightly wilted, about 2 minutes. Add vinegar and orange segments and reserved juice to the pan.

2. Transfer radicchio mixture to a large bowl. Add chicken, goat cheese, tarragon, and toasted bread or croutons. Toss to combine; season to taste with salt and pepper and serve.

1. Cut through the center of the breast down to the breast bone.

2. Remove breast halves. Pull legs away from the frame. Remove skin and pull meat away from leg bones, then pull meat into shreds or chunks.

SAUTÉED **CHICKEN** WINGS WITH KALE, CHERRY PEPPERS & PORK GRAVY

Chicken wings are dirt cheap and really, really tasty. If you love them Buffalo-style, you'll love them this way too. **makes 4 servings**

grocery list

fresh

1¾ pounds chicken wingettes

2 bunches kale

packaged

1-ounce package fresh thyme leaves

20-ounce can plum tomatoes

6-ounce bottle sliced hot cherry peppers

12-ounce jar Heinz® pork gravy

staples

vegetable oil

tools

large sauté pan

ingredients

2 tablespoons vegetable oil

1¾ pounds chicken wingettes
Salt and freshly ground pepper

3 tablespoons fresh thyme leaves, chopped

6 cups cleaned, roughly chopped kale

1 20-ounce can plum tomatoes, drained and roughly chopped

⅓ cup sliced hot cherry peppers, roughly chopped

1 12-ounce jar Heinz® pork gravy

method

1. In a large sauté pan heat oil over high heat. Season wings with salt and pepper and 2 tablespoons of the fresh thyme. Add to hot oil in pan. Cook wings until golden brown and just cooked through, 3 to 4 minutes per side. Remove from pan; cover lightly with foil to keep warm.

2. Drain off all but 2 tablespoons of the oil. Add the remaining tablespoon of thyme and kale to pan. Cover and cook, stirring occasionally, until kale is wilted and tender, about 6 minutes.

3. Add tomatoes, cherry peppers, and pork gravy to the pan and bring to simmer; season to taste with salt and pepper, if necessary. Serve chicken wings on top of kale mixture.

SPICY **TURKEY** PEPPERONI FRICASSEE OVER SOURDOUGH & PROVOLONE CROUTONS

Toasting the bread before you top it with turkey, sauce, and cheese keeps it crisp, so it crunches like a crouton when you bite into it. **makes 4 servings**

ingredients

4 large slices sourdough bread

7½ ounces link pepperoni, diced

1 24-ounce jar Bertolli® Tomato and Basil pasta sauce

1 pound turkey tenderloins or chicken tenders, cut into strips

Salt and freshly ground pepper

1 cup small pepperoncini, rough chopped

½ cup pitted kalamata olives, rough chopped

½ cup chopped fresh flat-leaf parsley

6 ounces grated provolone cheese

method

1. Preheat broiler on high. Line a rimmed baking sheet with foil. Toast bread under broiler until golden brown and a little crunchy, about 1 minute per side.

2. Meanwhile, heat pepperoni in a large sauté pan over medium heat. Cook until some of its fat is rendered and it is hot throughout.

3. Add pasta sauce to the pan; bring to a simmer. Season turkey generously with salt and pepper; add directly to the sauce. Simmer, stirring occasionally, until turkey is just cooked throughout, about 6 minutes. Stir in pepperoncini, olives, and parsley. Season to taste with salt and pepper, if necessary.

4. Spoon turkey mixture over bread slices; top with cheese. Broil until cheese is golden brown and bubbling, about 3 minutes. Serve immediately.

grocery list

fresh

7½ ounces link pepperoni

1 pound turkey tenderloins or chicken tenders

1 bunch flat-leaf parsley

packaged

1 loaf sourdough bread

24-ounce jar Bertolli® Tomato and Basil pasta sauce

12-ounce bottle pepperoncini

6-ounce jar pitted kalamata olives

6-ounce package provolone cheese

tools

rimmed baking sheet

large sauté pan

> " Bacon may be my favorite form of **PORK**—but there's lots to love in chops, cutlets, and tenderloins too. "

PORK CHOPS WOODSMAN-STYLE WITH POTATOES, PEPPERS & ROSEMARY

Woodsman-style, hunter-style, or alla cacciatore—all refer to the same thing: food flavored with the wonderful things you find in the forest, like juniper and rosemary. **makes 4 servings**

ingredients

- ½ cup Bertolli® extra-virgin olive oil
- 2 tablespoons Amore® garlic paste, or 6 garlic cloves, minced
- ⅓ cup chopped fresh rosemary leaves
- 1 tablespoon crushed juniper berries
- 4 bone-in pork chops, about 1¾ pounds total
- 2 large Idaho potatoes, scrubbed (leave peel on), quartered, and cut into ⅓-inch-thick slices
- 2 green peppers, stemmed, seeded, and cut into ½-inch-thick slices
- Salt and freshly ground pepper

method

1. Preheat oven to 450°F. Line a large rimmed baking sheet with foil.

2. Combine olive oil, garlic paste, rosemary, and juniper berries in a large bowl. Coat pork chops with about one-third of the oil mixture; set aside.

3. Add potatoes and peppers to the bowl; toss to coat. Season vegetables generously with salt and pepper. Scatter vegetables on the prepared baking sheet and roast for 15 minutes.

4. Remove pan from oven and turn broiler on high. Place pork chops on top of vegetables. Broil until vegetables begin to brown and pork is just cooked through, about 4 minutes per side.

5. Season pork chops to taste with salt and pepper, if necessary; serve chops with vegetables.

grocery list

fresh
4 bone-in pork chops (about 1¾ pounds)
2 large Idaho potatoes
2 green peppers

packaged
3.15-ounce tube Amore® garlic paste
½-ounce package fresh rosemary
1.3-ounce jar juniper berries

staples
extra-virgin olive oil

tools

rimmed baking sheet

CHUNKY **PORK** & PEPPER PIE WITH PUFF PASTRY

This is Pot Pie 101. You don't have to make the pastry, cook the pork, or even make the sauce.

makes 4 servings

grocery list

fresh
2 green peppers
1¾ pounds ham steak
1 bunch chives

packaged
14.5-ounce can sliced carrots
16-ounce package Imagine® Organic Creamy Potato Leek Soup
6-ounce container Old Bay® seasoning
17.3-ounce package frozen puff pastry sheets

staples
unsalted butter

tools

large sauté pan

8x12-inch glass baking dish

ingredients

4   tablespoons unsalted butter
2   green peppers, stemmed, seeded, and sliced thin
1   14.5-ounce can sliced carrots, drained
1½ cups Imagine® Organic Creamy Potato Leek Soup
1   tablespoon Old Bay® seasoning
1¾ pounds ham steak, cut into bite-size chunks
⅓   cup chopped chives
    Salt and freshly ground pepper
1   sheet frozen puff pastry, thawed

method

1. Preheat oven to 400°F.

2. In a large sauté pan heat butter over high heat until melted. Add peppers to pan. Cook, stirring occasionally, until peppers are tender, about 7 minutes.

3. Add carrots, potato-leek soup, and Old Bay® seasoning; bring to a simmer. Stir in ham and chives; season to taste with salt and pepper, if necessary.

4. Pour mixture into an 8×12-inch glass baking dish. Cut puff pastry to fit pan and place on top of pork mixture.

5. Bake until pastry is golden brown, about 30 minutes. Let stand 5 minutes before serving.

the fix
Burnt pastry? No problem. Cut it off and replace it with another one. The filling will be just fine. Luckily, puff pastry usually comes in boxes of two sheets. You might have to let it thaw at room temperature, but that doesn't take long. Check the box for thawing directions.

CREAMY CURRIED **PORK** & ZUCCHINI WITH CRUSHED CHICKPEAS

A spoonful of anything from India called "paste" or "pickles" will make you look like a rock star chef—but it will also add a lot of heat, so make sure you use those labeled "mild." **makes 4 servings**

ingredients

2   15-ounce cans chickpeas, rinsed and drained
⅓   cup Patak's® mild curry paste
1   24-ounce jar Bertolli® Vineyard Marinara pasta sauce
1¼ pounds pork tenderloin, cut into bite-size chunks
     Salt and freshly ground pepper
2   medium zucchini, cut in half horizontally and sliced into ⅓-inch half moons
1   cup Greek yogurt, preferably Fage®
1   cup chopped fresh cilantro
3   tablespoons Bertolli® extra-virgin olive oil

method

1. Put chickpeas in a large microwaveable bowl, cover with plastic wrap, and microwave on high until very hot, about 4 minutes.
2. Meanwhile, in a Dutch oven, heat curry paste over medium-high heat until fragrant. Add pasta sauce and stir to combine. Season pork with salt and pepper and stir into the pot, along with the zucchini. When mixture comes to a simmer, turn heat down to medium-low and cook, stirring often, until pork is cooked through and zucchini is tender, about 8 minutes. Stir in the yogurt and half of the cilantro. Season to taste with salt and pepper.
3. Season the hot chickpeas to taste with salt and pepper. Add the olive oil and remaining cilantro to the chickpeas. Roughly mash with a potato masher. Season to taste with salt and pepper, if necessary.
4. To serve, make a bed of the chickpeas on a serving platter and top with the pork curry.

grocery list

fresh

1¼ pounds pork tenderloin

2 medium zucchini

1 bunch cilantro

packaged

2 15-ounce cans chickpeas

10-ounce bottle Patak's® mild curry paste

24-ounce jar Bertolli® Vineyard Marinara pasta sauce

17.6-ounce container Fage® Total Greek yogurt

staples

extra-virgin olive oil

tools

large microwaveable bowl

Dutch oven

HOT & SOUR **PORK** STEW WITH NAPA CABBAGE

When I add lean, raw chunks or slices of meat to hot liquid, I always cook over low heat to keep the meat tender. Cooking it over high heat toughens it. **makes 4 servings**

grocery list

fresh

1 large head napa cabbage

1½ pounds pork tenderloin

packaged

8.5-ounce bottle Kikkoman® tamari soy sauce

19-ounce jar duck sauce

8-ounce package shiitake mushrooms

7-ounce bottle A Taste of Thai® garlic chili pepper sauce

staples

low-sodium chicken broth

rice wine vinegar

tools

large saucepan

ingredients

2   14.5-ounce cans low-sodium chicken broth

½   cup Kikkoman® tamari soy sauce

¼   cup duck sauce

1   large head napa cabbage, halved and cut crosswise into ¼-inch strips, about 9 cups

8   ounces shiitake mushrooms, stems removed, sliced

1½ pounds pork tenderloin, sliced thin

     Salt and freshly ground pepper

3   tablespoons rice wine vinegar

2   tablespoons A Taste of Thai® garlic chili pepper sauce

method

1. In a large saucepan bring chicken broth, tamari, and duck sauce to boiling over medium heat. Add napa cabbage and mushrooms; cover and simmer until cabbage and mushrooms are tender, about 4 minutes.

2. Turn heat down to low. Season pork with salt and pepper and add to the broth. Cook, stirring occasionally, until pork is just cooked through, 2 to 3 minutes.

3. Stir in vinegar and chili sauce; season to taste with salt and pepper, if necessary, and serve.

FRIED **PORK** & BEANS

Pork and beans straight from the can was one of my faves as a kid. This slightly juiced-up version is just a tad better, I think. **makes 4 servings**

ingredients

2   tablespoons vegetable oil
1½ pounds boneless pork chops
     Salt and freshly ground
     pepper
½   pound thick-cut bacon, cut
     into lardons (see how-to
     photos, page 73)
1   12-ounce jar Mancini® fried
     peppers
1   28-ounce can peeled
     tomatoes, drained and
     roughly chopped, ½ cup
     juice reserved
⅔   cup ketchup
2   15-ounce cans red kidney
     beans, rinsed and drained

method

1. In a large cast-iron skillet heat oil over medium-high heat. Season pork chops with salt and pepper; add to the pan. Cook until golden brown and just cooked through, about 4 minutes per side. Remove from pan; cover lightly with foil to keep warm.

2. Add bacon to the pan and cook, stirring occasionally, until golden brown but not crisp, about 5 to 6 minutes. Drain off half of the fat. Add peppers, tomatoes, reserved juice, ketchup, and beans to the pan; bring to a simmer.

3. Season to taste with salt and pepper, if necessary. Serve bean mixture with pork chops.

grocery list

fresh

1½ pounds boneless
pork chops

½ pound thick-cut bacon

packaged

12-ounce jar Mancini®
fried peppers

28-ounce can peeled
tomatoes

2 15-ounce cans red
kidney beans

staples

vegetable oil

ketchup

tools

large cast-iron skillet

GRUYÈRE-STUFFED **PORK** WITH GARLICKY WILD MUSHROOMS & SPINACH

The designation of a dish as "garlicky" essentially means that it might be hazardous to your social life. I'm always willing to give up a kiss here and there for anything "garlicky." **makes 4 servings**

grocery list

fresh

1¼ pounds pork tenderloin

packaged

8-ounce package Gruyère cheese

12-ounce package sliced wild mushrooms

3.15-ounce tube Amore® garlic paste

9-ounce package fresh baby spinach

staples

extra-virgin olive oil

butter

crushed red pepper

tools

rimmed baking sheet

large cast-iron skillet

ingredients

1¼ pounds pork tenderloin, cut into 4 portions and pounded to about ¼ inch thick

8   1-ounce slices Gruyère cheese

2   tablespoons Bertolli® extra-virgin olive oil
    Salt and freshly ground pepper

4   tablespoons butter

1   12-ounce package sliced wild mushrooms

3   tablespoons Amore® garlic paste, or 9 garlic cloves, chopped

½   teaspoon crushed red pepper

1   9-ounce package fresh baby spinach

method

1. Preheat broiler on high. Line a rimmed baking sheet with foil.
2. Lay pork on a work surface. Lay 2 slices of cheese on one half of each piece of pork. Fold pork over to cover the cheese; secure each package with a toothpick. Coat pork with olive oil and season generously with salt and pepper. Place on the prepared baking sheet and broil until pork is just cooked through and golden brown and cheese is melted, 4 to 5 minutes per side.
3. Meanwhile, in a large cast-iron skillet or sauté pan heat butter over medium-high heat. When butter begins to brown, add mushrooms. Cook, stirring occasionally, until mushrooms are golden brown, about 4 to 5 minutes. Stir garlic paste thoroughly into mushroom mixture. Continue to cook, stirring, until garlic is fragrant, about 1 to 2 more minutes. Stir in crushed red pepper. Add spinach to the pan. Season generously with salt and pepper. Cover and cook until spinach is wilted, about 3 more minutes
4. Season to taste with salt and pepper, if necessary. Serve pork on a bed of the spinach-mushroom mixture.

CURRIED BROILED **PORK** CHOPS WITH DIRTY RICE

Dirty rice from the South is almost always made with white rice and those bird bits that are euphemistically called giblets (don't ask). I created this version to have the same look and great flavor without them. **makes 4 servings**

grocery list

fresh

4 bone-in pork chops (about 1¾ pounds)

packaged

10-ounce bottle Patak's® mild curry paste

3.15-ounce tube Amore® garlic paste

12-ounce jar Victoria® hot dog onions

12-ounce jar Mancini® fried peppers

Two 8.8-ounce packages Uncle Ben's® Original Long-Grain White Ready Rice®

staples

extra-virgin olive oil

limes

tools

rimmed baking sheet

ingredients

3 tablespoons Patak's® mild curry paste

⅓ cup plus 1 tablespoon Bertolli® extra-virgin olive oil

4 bone-in pork chops, about 1¾ pounds total
Salt and freshly ground pepper
Juice of 1½ limes

2 tablespoons Amore® garlic paste, or 6 garlic cloves, chopped

1 12-ounce jar Victoria® hot dog onions

1 12-ounce jar Mancini® fried peppers

2 8.8-ounce packages Uncle Ben's® Original Long-Grain White Ready Rice®

method

1. Preheat broiler on high. Line a rimmed baking sheet with foil.
2. Combine curry paste and the ⅓ cup olive oil. Coat chops in 3 tablespoons of this mixture. Season pork with salt and pepper. Place on prepared baking sheet and broil until just cooked through, about 6 minutes per side.
3. Meanwhile, add lime juice to remaining curry mixture to make a vinaigrette; season to taste with salt and pepper and set aside.
4. Heat the remaining tablespoon olive oil in a large sauté pan over medium heat. Add garlic paste and cook, stirring to break up, until garlic is pale golden, 2 to 3 minutes. Add hot dog onions and peppers to the pan and cook until hot throughout, about 3 minutes.
5. While peppers and onions cook, heat rice in microwave in pouches according to package directions. Transfer to a large bowl; stir in peppers and onions; season to taste with salt and pepper.
6. Make a bed of the rice mixture on a platter and lay pork chops on top. Spoon curry vinaigrette over pork chops and rice and serve.

PORK & CARROT STEW WITH CURRY LIME & CILANTRO BROTH

By dividing the ground pork into small chunks and cooking it in the hot broth, you get little meatballs without any tedious rolling. By highly seasoning the broth, you don't have to season the meatballs.

makes 4 servings

ingredients

½ cup Patak's® mild curry paste

3 tablespoons chopped fresh ginger

2 14-ounce cans low-sodium chicken broth

2 cups crinkle-cut sliced fresh carrots, such as Grimmway Farms® Carrot Chips™

1½ pounds ground pork, divided into 24 equal chunks

Salt and freshly ground pepper

2 15-ounce cans chickpeas, rinsed and drained

Juice of 2 limes

1 cup chopped fresh cilantro

method

1. In a large soup pot or Dutch oven heat curry paste and ginger over medium heat, stirring frequently, until very fragrant and slightly toasted, about 2 minutes.
2. Stir in chicken broth and bring to a simmer. Add carrots. Cover and simmer until carrots are just tender, about 8 minutes. Season pork with salt and pepper and gently add chunks to the pot. Lower the heat to a very low simmer. Cover and cook until pork is just cooked through, 3 to 4 minutes.
3. Add chickpeas, lime juice, and cilantro to the pot. Continue to cook for another 2 minutes or until chickpeas are hot.
4. Season to taste with salt and pepper, if necessary, and serve.

grocery list

fresh

1½ pounds ground pork

1 bunch cilantro

packaged

10-ounce jar Patak's® mild curry paste

1-inch piece fresh ginger

1 pound bag Grimmway Farms® Carrot Chips™

Two 15-ounce cans chickpeas

staples

low-sodium chicken broth

limes

tools

Dutch oven

PORK CHOPS WITH ONIONS & NOODLES

This is comfort food, defined: crispy, pan-fried pork chops on a bed of egg noodles tossed with gravy and sweet, caramelized onions. **makes 4 servings**

grocery list

fresh

4 bone-in pork chops (about 1¾ pounds)

1 bunch flat-leaf parsley

packaged

12-ounce package wide egg noodles

12-ounce jar Heinz® pork gravy

staples

vegetable oil

unsalted butter

Vidalia onions

tools

stockpot

large cast-iron skillet

ingredients

12 ounces wide egg noodles
2 tablespoons vegetable oil
4 bone-in pork chops, about 1¾ pounds total
Salt and freshly ground pepper
½ cup unsalted butter
2 large Vidalia onions, thinly sliced
1 12-ounce jar Heinz® pork gravy
¾ cup chopped fresh flat-leaf parsley

method

1. Bring a stockpot of salted water to a boil. Cook egg noodles according to package directions, about 8 minutes.

2. Meanwhile, in a large cast-iron skillet heat oil over medium-high heat. Season pork chops generously with salt and pepper. Cook until golden brown and just cooked through, about 4 minutes per side. Remove from pan; cover lightly with foil to keep warm.

3. Add butter to the pan. When butter is foamy, add onions to the pan. Cook, stirring occasionally, until onions are golden brown and tender, about 15 minutes. Add gravy to the onions. Season to taste with salt and pepper.

4. Toss onion mixture with cooked noodles and parsley. Season to taste with salt and pepper, if necessary. Serve pork chops on a bed of noodles.

SAUTÉED **PORK** CUTLETS WITH APPLES, COLLARD GREENS & BACON

Finding these great fried apples inspired me to do a quick-and-easy take on what's traditionally a slow-cooked Southern dish. Look for collard greens that are already cut and cleaned. **makes 4 servings**

ingredients

2 tablespoons vegetable oil
4 thin pork cutlets, about
   1½ pounds total
   Salt and freshly ground
   pepper
½ pound thick-cut bacon, sliced
   into lardons (see how-to
   photos, page 73)
3 tablespoons Amore®
   garlic paste, or 9 garlic
   cloves, chopped
1 large head collard greens,
   cleaned and roughly
   chopped (about 6 cups)
1 28-ounce jar Lucky Leaf®
   Fried Apples
½ cup Dijon mustard

method

1. In a large cast-iron skillet heat oil over high heat. Season pork with salt and pepper; add to the pan. Cook until golden brown and just cooked through, about 3 minutes per side. Remove from pan; cover lightly with foil to keep warm.
2. Add bacon to the pan and cook, stirring occasionally, until golden brown but not crisp, 5 or 6 minutes. Add garlic paste and cook, stirring to break up, for another minute. Add collard greens; season with salt and pepper to taste. Cover and cook, stirring once or twice, until collards are tender, about 5 minutes.
3. Add apples to the pan and cover. Cook until apples are hot throughout, 3 to 4 minutes. Stir in mustard; season to taste with salt and pepper, if necessary.
4. Serve cutlets with apple and collard mixture.

grocery list

fresh

4 thin pork cutlets (about
   1½ pounds)

½ pound thick-cut bacon

1 head collard greens

packaged

3.15-ounce tube Amore®
   garlic paste

28-ounce jar Lucky Leaf®
   Fried Apples

staples

vegetable oil

Dijon mustard

tools

large cast-iron skillet

PORK & BOK CHOY STIR FRY WITH SPICY PEANUT SAUCE

I know, at first glance it seems bizarre—but grapefruit and peanut sauce are really good together. The acidity of the citrus balances out the richness of the sauce. **makes 4 servings**

ingredients

2   8.8-ounce packages Uncle Ben's® Long-Grain White Ready Rice®
3   tablespoons vegetable oil
1½ pounds pork loin, cut into strips
    Salt and freshly ground pepper
1   large head bok choy, washed and roughly chopped, about 6 cups
1   11.5-ounce bottle House of Tsang® Bangkok Padang peanut sauce
3   large ruby grapefruits, peeled and segmented (see page 78)
½   cup chopped fresh cilantro

method

1. Heat rice in microwave in pouches according to package directions.
2. Meanwhile, in a large cast-iron skillet or sauté pan heat 2 tablespoons of the vegetable oil over high heat.
3. Season pork with salt and pepper and add to the pan. Cook, stirring frequently, until pork is golden brown and just cooked through, about 5 minutes. Remove pork from the pan; cover lightly with foil to keep warm.
4. Add remaining tablespoon of oil to the pan. When oil is hot, add bok choy. Season to taste with salt and pepper and cook, stirring frequently, until tender, about 5 minutes. Add peanut sauce and bring to a simmer.
5. Return pork to the pan and stir in grapefruit and cilantro. Season to taste with salt and pepper, if necessary, and serve over hot rice.

grocery list

fresh

1½ pounds pork loin

1 large head bok choy

3 large ruby grapefruits

1 bunch cilantro

packaged

Two 8.8-ounce packages Uncle Ben's® Long-Grain White Ready Rice®

11.5-ounce bottle House of Tsang® Bangkok Padang peanut sauce

staples

vegetable oil

tools

large cast-iron skillet

PORK CUTLETS WITH SNAP PEAS, MUSHROOMS & SHERRY

Pork cutlets cooked in an egg batter like this make a great base for all kinds of menus. You could serve them simply with two lemon wedges and a little salad, or with any one or two favorite side dishes.

makes 4 servings

grocery list

fresh

1½ pounds pork cutlets

packaged

Two 8-ounce containers wild mushrooms

8-ounce package sugar snap peas

staples

unsalted butter

flour

eggs

sherry

tools

large sauté pan

ingredients

1   cup unsalted butter (16 tablespoons)
1½ pounds pork cutlets
1   cup all-purpose flour, for dredging
2   eggs, lightly beaten
    Salt and freshly ground pepper
12 ounces wild mushrooms
1   8-ounce package sugar snap peas
1   cup dry sherry

method

1. In a large sauté pan, heat 6 tablespoons butter over high heat until foamy and golden brown. Meanwhile, dredge cutlets first in flour, then in the beaten eggs. Add to the pan. Cook cutlets until golden and just cooked through, 2 to 3 minutes per side. Remove from pan. Season to taste with salt and pepper; cover lightly with foil to keep warm. Wipe inside of pan with a clean paper towel.
2. Add 4 tablespoons butter to the pan. When foamy and golden brown, add the mushrooms. Cook, stirring occasionally, until mushrooms are golden brown, about 6 minutes. Add snap peas. Season to taste with salt and pepper. Cook, stirring occasionally, for another 3 minutes.
3. Add sherry and simmer until reduced by half. Add remaining butter and swirl to incorporate into the sauce. Spoon vegetable mixture over the pork cutlets and serve.

PORK ENCHILADAS WITH CHEESE & TOMATILLO SALSA

Between the Ready Rice®, the smoked ham, and the jarred salsa, you've got very little to do here—and very few excuses left. Turn on the stove and char a few tortillas, and it looks like you did it all yourself.

makes 4 servings

ingredients

4   large flour tortillas
2   8.8-ounce packages Uncle Ben's® Santa Fe Ready Rice®
1   pound Smithfield® ham, diced
    Juice of 2 limes
1   cup chopped fresh cilantro
12 ounces shredded white cheddar, about 3 cups
    Salt and freshly ground pepper
1   16-ounce jar Salpica™ Cilantro Green Olive Salsa
    Sour cream, for serving

method

1. Preheat oven to 375°F.

2. Turn a stovetop burner on high. Lay the tortillas, one at a time, directly on the burner to lightly char, about 45 seconds per side. Set aside.

3. In a medium microwaveable bowl, combine rice and diced ham. Cover with plastic wrap and microwave on high until warm, about 3 minutes. Stir in lime juice, half of the cilantro, and 1 cup of the cheddar cheese. Season to taste with salt and pepper.

4. On a work surface, lay out the tortillas. Divide the rice mixture among the four tortillas. Working with one tortilla at a time, fold the opposite sides of the tortilla toward the center so that the filling is almost completely covered. Starting at the bottom, roll the tortilla into a tight enchilada "package." Place enchilada, seam side down, into a 9×13-inch baking dish. Repeat with remaining tortillas. Pour salsa over the top of the tortillas and top with remaining cheese.

5. Bake until cheese is bubbling and filling is hot throughout, about 20 minutes. Sprinkle remaining cilantro over the top of the enchiladas; serve with sour cream.

grocery list

fresh

1 pound Smithfield® ham

1 bunch cilantro

packaged

Two 8.8-ounce packages Uncle Ben's® Santa Fe Ready Rice®

12-ounce package shredded white cheddar cheese

16-ounce Salpica™ Cilantro Green Olive Salsa

8-count package large flour tortillas

staples

limes

sour cream

tools

medium microwaveable bowl

9x13-inch baking dish

PORK & POTATO DUMPLINGS WITH CREAMY SMOKED PAPRIKA SAUCE

Cheater alert: I'm calling purchased gnocchi "potato dumplings" because that's exactly what they are. No one said you had to make them yourself. **makes 4 servings**

grocery list

fresh

1½ pounds boneless pork chops

1 bunch chives

packaged

24-ounce package fresh potato gnocchi

1.62-ounce bottle sweet smoked paprika

staples

vegetable oil

unsalted butter

Vidalia onion

sour cream

tools

large cast-iron skillet

stockpot

ingredients

2 tablespoons vegetable oil
1½ pounds boneless pork chops
 Salt and freshly ground pepper
1½ pounds fresh potato gnocchi
4 tablespoons unsalted butter
1 large Vidalia onion, sliced thin
1 tablespoon plus 1 teaspoon sweet smoked paprika (also called pimentón)
1½ cups sour cream
⅓ cup chopped fresh chives

method

1. In a large cast-iron skillet, heat vegetable oil over high heat. Season pork chops with salt and pepper; add to the pan. Cook until golden brown and just cooked through, about 4 minutes per side. Remove from pan; cover lightly with foil to keep warm. Turn heat to medium high.

2. While pork is cooking, bring a stockpot of salted water to a boil and cook gnocchi according to package directions. Reserve ½ cup of the cooking water when gnocchi are done.

3. After pork chops are cooked, add butter to the pan over medium-high heat. When butter is hot, add onion. Season with salt and pepper. Cook, stirring occasionally, until onions are tender and caramelized, about 12 minutes.

4. Add the paprika, sour cream, gnocchi, and reserved gnocchi-cooking water to the pan; toss to coat. Stir in chives; season to taste with salt and pepper, if necessary.

5. Serve pork chops with gnocchi mixture.

the fix

Smoked paprika has an assertive flavor—even the sweet stuff (there's also picante, or hot). That's why I love it. But if you find you've added too much—or it's too much for your taste, just add some more sour cream to soften the flavor.

PORK PARMIGIANO WITH CAPONATA & ROSEMARY

I just keep on reinventing the dish we all know and love as "parmigiano." It's the Italian-American recipe gift that keeps on giving. In this version, the caponata—a Sicilian sweet and sour eggplant relish—really sets it apart. **makes 4 servings**

grocery list

fresh

1½ pounds thin pork cutlets

packaged

Two 13.5-ounce pouches Bertolli® Premium Sun-Ripened Tomato & Olive pasta sauce

Two 7.5-ounce jars Paesana™ caponata

1-ounce package fresh rosemary

Two 8-ounce packages shredded whole milk mozzarella cheese

staples

eggs

plain breadcrumbs

vegetable oil

tools

large sauté pan

9x13-inch glass baking dish

ingredients

1½ pounds thin pork cutlets
2 eggs, beaten
2 cups plain breadcrumbs
½ cup vegetable oil
  Salt and freshly ground pepper
2 13.5-ounce pouches Bertolli® Premium Sun-Ripened Tomato & Olive pasta sauce
2 7.5-ounce jars Paesana™ caponata
2 tablespoons chopped fresh rosemary
12 ounces shredded whole milk mozzarella, about 3 cups

method

1. Preheat oven to 400°F.
2. Dip cutlets in egg and then in breadcrumbs to coat.
3. Meanwhile, in a large sauté pan heat vegetable oil over medium-high heat. Cook cutlets until golden brown, about 2 minutes per side. Drain on a cooling rack or on a paper towel-lined plate. Season to taste with salt and pepper.
4. Spread 1 pouch of the pasta sauce over the bottom of a 9×13-inch glass baking dish. Lay the cutlets on top of sauce. Top cutlets with remaining pouch of pasta sauce and caponata. Sprinkle rosemary and cheese over the top.
5. Bake until cheese is melted and dish is hot throughout, 15 to 20 minutes.

PORK SCALOPPINE WITH MUSHROOM & RED WINE SAUCE

A scaloppine is a thin slice of meat that's sautéed quickly and served with a sauce made in the same pan. If you can't find very thin cutlets, pound them a little with a meat mallet before cooking them.

makes 4 servings

ingredients

2 8.8-ounce packages Uncle Ben's® Vegetable Harvest Ready Whole Grain Medley™

4 thin pork cutlets, about 1½ pounds
   Salt and freshly ground pepper

1 cup all-purpose flour, for dredging

1 cup unsalted butter (16 tablespoons)

2 large shallots, thinly sliced

12 ounces sliced button mushrooms

2 tablespoons fresh thyme leaves

1½ cups dry red wine

method

1. Heat rice in microwave in pouch according to package directions.
2. Meanwhile, season pork with salt and pepper; dredge in flour. In a large cast-iron skillet heat 4 tablespoons butter over medium heat until foamy and golden brown. Add cutlets to the pan; cook until just cooked through, 1 to 2 minutes per side. Remove from pan; cover lightly with aluminum foil to keep warm. Wipe out the pan with a clean paper towel.
3. Add 4 tablespoons of butter to the pan; when butter is foamy, add shallots. Cook, stirring, for about 1 minute or until shallots are fragrant and starting to get tender. Add mushrooms and thyme and cook, stirring occasionally, until mushrooms are tender, about 5 minutes. Season to taste with salt and pepper.
4. Add wine; let simmer until reduced by half. Add remaining 8 tablespoons butter to the mushrooms. Gently swirl pan to incorporate butter into the sauce.
5. Season sauce to taste with salt and pepper, if necessary. On a serving platter, make a bed of rice and top with pork cutlets. Spoon the red wine-mushroom sauce over the pork and serve.

grocery list

fresh

4 thin cut pork cutlets (about 1½ pounds)

2 large shallots

packaged

Two 8.8-ounce packages Uncle Ben's® Vegetable Harvest Ready Whole Grain Medley™

Two 8-ounce packages sliced button mushrooms

1-ounce package fresh thyme leaves

staples

flour

unsalted butter

dry red wine

tools

large cast-iron skillet

PORK CORDON BLEU WITH CHUNKY MUSHROOM SAUCE

"Cordon bleu" literally means "blue ribbon" in French, but culinarily speaking, it refers to the humblest but most delicious flavor combination: ham and cheese. This is basically a ham and cheese sandwhich that swaps the bread for pork cutlets. **makes 4 servings**

ingredients

1¼ pounds thin pork cutlets, 8 pieces
4 ounces cooked ham
6 ounces sliced Swiss cheese
2 eggs, lightly beaten
2 cups Japanese panko breadcrumbs
   Salt and freshly ground pepper
1 18-ounce can Progresso® Creamy Mushroom Soup
2 cups Bertolli® Premium Champignon & Portobello Mushroom pasta sauce
8 ounces sliced wild mushrooms

method

1. Preheat oven to 400°F. Line a rimmed baking sheet with foil.
2. Lay 4 pork cutlets on a work surface. Divide ham and cheese slices evenly among the cutlets. Top each cutlet with another cutlet.
3. Gently dip each pork bundle in egg and then in breadcrumbs to coat. Place on the prepared baking sheet. Season with salt and pepper.
4. Bake until golden brown and cheese is melted, about 20 minutes.
5. Meanwhile, in a medium saucepan, bring soup, pasta sauce, and mushrooms to a simmer over medium-high heat. Simmer until mushrooms are tender and sauce is slightly reduced, about 8 minutes.
6. Season mushroom sauce with salt and pepper to taste and spoon over the pork to serve.

grocery list

fresh

1¼ pounds thin pork cutlets

4 ounces cooked ham

packaged

7-ounce package Japanese panko breadcrumbs

Two 13.5-ounce pouches Bertolli® Premium Champignon & Portobello Mushroom pasta sauce

8-ounce package sliced Swiss cheese

18-ounce can Progresso® Creamy Mushroom Soup

8-ounce package sliced wild mushrooms

staples

eggs

tools

rimmed baking sheet

PORK SHEPHERD'S PIE

Shepherd's pie is the traditional English way of using leftover roasted meat—usually lamb—with mashed potatoes as an easy pie crust. Here I've turned it into a pork fest with bacon, sausage, and ground pork shoulder. Yum! **makes 4 servings**

grocery list

fresh

¼ pound bacon

1 pound ground pork

2 links hot Italian sausage

packaged

2-pound container Diner's Choice® Garlic Mashed Potatoes

7-ounce jar cocktail onions

12-ounce jar Mancini® fried peppers

12-ounce package sharp white cheddar cheese

staples

tools

large cast-iron skillet

9x13-inch glass baking dish

ingredients

1   2-pound container Diner's Choice® Garlic Mashed Potatoes

¼   pound bacon, cut into lardons (see how-to photos, page 73)

1   pound ground pork

2   links hot Italian sausage, casing removed

1   7-ounce jar cocktail onions, drained

1   12-ounce jar Mancini® fried peppers

    Salt and freshly ground pepper

12 ounces grated sharp white cheddar cheese, about 3 cups

method

1. Preheat oven to 375°F. Heat potatoes in microwave according to package directions.

2. Meanwhile, heat a large cast-iron skillet over medium-high heat. Add bacon and cook, stirring occasionally, until golden brown, about 5 minutes.

3. Add ground pork and sausage. Cook, breaking up the meat with a wooden spoon and stirring occasionally, until cooked through, about 6 minutes.

4. Drain fat. Add onions and peppers. When vegetables are hot, season to taste with salt and pepper.

5. Spread pork and vegetable mixture in the bottom of a 9×13-inch glass baking dish. Spread mashed potatoes evenly over top of pork to the edges of the pan.

6. Sprinkle cheese on top and bake until cheddar is melted and dish is hot throughout, about 15 minutes.

PORK STIR-FRY WITH SPICY PLUM SAUCE, MUSTARD GREENS & RICE

Plum sauce is a thick, light brown sweet and sour paste used in Chinese cooking. In this dish I also tossed in dried plums, a.k.a. "prunes," which make it taste truly plummy. **makes 4 servings**

ingredients

2   8.8-ounce packages Uncle Ben's® Original Long Grain Ready Rice®
3   tablespoons vegetable oil
1¼ pounds pork cutlets, cut into strips
    Salt and freshly ground pepper
1   head mustard greens, cleaned and roughly chopped, about 6 cups
1   10-ounce jar plum sauce
3   tablespoons A Taste of Thai® garlic chili pepper sauce
1   10-ounce package Sunsweet® pitted prunes, rough chopped

method

1. Heat rice in pouches according to package directions.
2. Meanwhile, heat 2 tablespoons of the oil in a large cast-iron skillet or sauté pan over high heat. Season pork with salt and pepper. Add pork to the pan and cook, stirring occasionally, until golden brown and cooked through, about 5 minutes. Remove pork from pan; cover lightly with foil to keep warm.
3. Add remaining tablespoon oil to the pan. When oil is hot, add mustard greens. Cook, stirring almost constantly, until mustard greens are wilted, about 3 minutes. Season to taste with salt and pepper.
4. Add plum sauce and chili sauce. When sauce begins to simmer, add prunes. Return pork to the pan and season to taste with salt and pepper, if necessary. Serve stir-fry over hot rice.

grocery list

fresh

1¼ pounds pork cutlets

1 head mustard greens

packaged

Two 8.8-ounce packages Uncle Ben's® Original Long Grain Ready Rice®

10-ounce jar plum sauce

7-ounce jar A Taste of Thai® garlic chili pepper sauce

10-ounce package Sunsweet® pitted prunes

staples

vegetable oil

tools

large cast-iron skillet

SMOKED **PORK** LOIN MEDALLIONS WITH LEEK & POTATO STEW

Smoking meat takes hours—but the payoff is great flavor and a tender texture. Good-quality smoked pork chops like these give you a running start on a super-fast dinner that only tastes slow-cooked.

makes 4 servings

grocery list

fresh

Two 11.5-ounce packages Smithfield® boneless smoked pork chops

2 leeks

2 large Idaho potatoes

1 bunch chives

packaged

Two 16-ounce containers Imagine® Organic Creamy Leek and Potato Soup

12-ounce jar Mancini® fried peppers

staples

unsalted butter

tools

Dutch oven

ingredients

1½ 11.5-ounce packages Smithfield® boneless smoked pork chops

4 tablespoons unsalted butter

2 leeks, washed, halved horizontally, and sliced crosswise into ¼-inch-thick slices (see how-to photos, page 109)

Salt and freshly ground pepper

2 large Idaho potatoes, peeled, quartered, and cut crosswise into ¼-inch-thick slices

2 16-ounce containers Imagine® Organic Creamy Leek and Potato Soup

1 12-ounce jar Mancini® fried peppers

⅓ cup chopped fresh chives

method

1. Preheat oven to 350°F. Heat pork chops according to package directions.
2. Meanwhile, in a Dutch oven heat butter over medium-high heat. When butter is melted and beginning to foam, add leeks; season to taste with salt and pepper. Cook, stirring occasionally, until leeks begin to soften, about 3 minutes.
3. Add potatoes. Continue to cook, stirring occasionally, until potatoes are almost tender, about 5 minutes. Add soup; cover and bring to a simmer.
4. Turn heat to low and simmer until potatoes and leeks are completely tender, about 6 minutes. Stir in peppers and chives; season to taste with salt and pepper, if necessary.
5. To serve, lay pork on a serving platter. Spoon potato, leek, and pepper mixture over the pork.

1. Begin by cutting the root end off of each leek with a sharp knife. Discard root.

2. Cut the tough dark green tops off the leeks, leaving only the light green and white portions. Discard the green top leaves.

3. Cut a shallow slice through the outer peel of the leeks

4. Remove the top layer of each leek and discard.

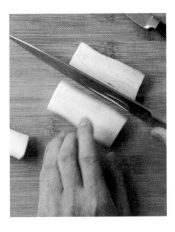

5. Cut the leeks in half lengthwise.

6. Thoroughly rinse the leek halves in cool water, fanning the layers apart. This allows water to wash the soil from between layers.

“
Don't be intimidated by **FISH**. It's actually very simple and quick to cook, full of interesting flavors, and fantastically good for you.
”

BARBECUE SALMON WITH BLACK BEANS & GRITS

Salmon does really well on the barbecue. It's a high-fat fish (the good kind!) with a mild, slightly sweet flavor that partners well with the tangy, vinegary barbecue sauces we all love. **makes 4 servings**

ingredients

4   6- to 8-ounce salmon steaks
    Salt and freshly ground
    pepper
1   14-ounce can black beans,
    rinsed and drained
1   cup barbecue sauce
¾   cup chunky applesauce
2   tablespoons cider vinegar
2½ cups whole milk
½   bunch scallions, sliced
    thin on a bias (see how-to
    photos, page 21)
⅔   cup instant grits

method

1. Preheat grill/grill pan/broiler on high. (If using the broiler, line a rimmed baking sheet with aluminum foil; lay the salmon on the prepared baking sheet.) Season salmon generously with salt and pepper. Grill or broil until just cooked through, about 3 minutes per side.
2. Meanwhile, in a large saucepan, combine beans, barbecue sauce, applesauce, and vinegar. Bring to a simmer over medium heat; season to taste with salt and pepper. Turn heat down to low to keep warm.
3. In a medium saucepan bring milk and scallions to a boil over high heat. Gradually whisk grits into milk. Turn heat down to low and cook, stirring often, until grits are tender, about 10 minutes. Season to taste with salt and pepper.
4. Pour grits into a large serving bowl. Top with salmon steaks and spoon barbecue beans over top of salmon.

grocery list

fresh

Four 6- to 8-ounce salmon steaks

1 bunch scallions

packaged

14-ounce can black beans

18-ounce bottle barbecue sauce

24-ounce jar chunky applesauce

12-ounce box instant grits

staples

cider vinegar

whole milk

tools

grill pan

1 large and
1 medium saucepan

SALMON WITH CHILI-LIME MARMALADE, RED PEPPERS & WATER CHESTNUTS

The flavor combination of chili and lime is everywhere these days. A hint of sweetness (here, it comes from apricot preserves) takes it to another level. **makes 4 servings**

grocery list

fresh
Four 6-ounce portions salmon fillet

2 large red peppers

packaged
12-ounce jar apricot preserves

8-ounce jar chili-garlic paste

13.5-ounce can sliced water chestnuts

staples
limes

vegetable oil

Vidalia onion

tools

rimmed baking sheet

large sauté pan

ingredients

1 cup apricot preserves
Juice of 2 limes
2 tablespoons chili-garlic paste
4 6-ounce portions salmon fillet
Salt and freshly ground pepper
2 tablespoons vegetable oil
2 large red peppers, stemmed, seeded, and sliced
1 large Vidalia onion, sliced thin
1 13.5-ounce can sliced water chestnuts, drained

method

1. Preheat oven to 375°F. Line a rimmed baking sheet with foil.
2. Combine apricot preserves, lime juice, and chili-garlic paste. Place salmon on prepared baking sheet. Glaze with half of the apricot mixture; season generously with salt and pepper. Bake until salmon is just cooked through, about 12 minutes.
3. Meanwhile, heat vegetable oil in a large sauté pan over high heat. Add peppers and onion to the pan. Season generously with salt and pepper; cook, stirring occasionally, until vegetables are tender, 5 to 6 minutes.
4. Add water chestnuts and remaining half of apricot glaze to the pan. Bring mixture to a simmer; season to taste with salt and pepper, if necessary.
5. Serve salmon on a bed of the vegetables.

the fix
Because it is generally lean, fish can go from perfectly done to dried out in a matter of minutes. If you find that you've overbaked your fish, you can compensate for the dryness by drizzling it with some additional apricot preserves, warmed up for a few seconds in the microwave.

SALMON & ARTICHOKES WITH PESTO & MASHED POTATOES

Artichokes have a natural butteriness to them and are really good for you. But who wants to clean them on a weeknight? Not me. That's why I use good-quality jarred, marinated artichokes.

makes 4 servings

ingredients

4 5-ounce portions salmon fillet
2 tablespoons Bertolli® extra-virgin olive oil
   Salt and freshly ground pepper
2 7-ounce jars marinated artichoke hearts
1 7.5-ounce jar pesto, preferably Paesana™ brand
1 cup grape tomatoes, halved
1 2-pound package Diner's Choice® garlic mashed potatoes

method

1. Preheat oven to 375°F.
2. Tear off a 16-inch-long sheet of aluminum foil and lay it on a rimmed baking sheet. Coat salmon with the olive oil and season generously with salt and pepper. Place salmon portions in the center of foil, spaced 1 to 2 inches apart.
3. In a medium bowl combine artichokes and their liquid, pesto, and tomatoes. Season with salt and pepper. Top salmon with artichoke mixture and cover with another 16-inch-long sheet of aluminum foil. Fold up edges of the foil to seal into a tight package. Bake until vegetables are hot and salmon is just cooked through, about 20 minutes.
4. Meanwhile, heat potatoes in microwave until hot, according to package directions.
5. Serve salmon and artichoke mixture on a bed of mashed potatoes.

grocery list

fresh

Four 5-ounce portions salmon fillet

1 pint grape tomatoes

packaged

Two 7-ounce jars marinated artichoke hearts

7.5-ounce jar Paesana™ pesto sauce

2-pound package Diner's Choice® garlic mashed potatoes

staples

extra-virgin olive oil

tools

rimmed baking sheet

FRESH & SMOKED SALMON CAKES WITH CHICKPEAS & TANGY GREEN SALAD

Combining fresh salmon with smoked salmon adds layers of flavor without having to run around looking for exotic ingredients. **makes 4 servings**

grocery list

fresh

⅔ pound salmon

8 ounces smoked salmon

packaged

15-ounce can chickpeas

8-ounce bottle Annie's Naturals® Lemon & Chive Dressing

1-pound bag chickpea flour

1-ounce package fresh thyme

10-ounce bag Dole® Italian Salad Mix

staples

vegetable oil

mayonnaise

tools

large sauté pan

ingredients

½ cup vegetable oil

⅔ pound salmon, finely chopped

8 ounces smoked salmon, finely chopped

1 cup chickpeas, rinsed and drained and finely chopped

½ cup mayonnaise

¼ cup plus 1 tablespoon prepared lemon vinaigrette, such as Annie's Naturals® Lemon & Chive Dressing

Salt and freshly ground pepper

1 cup chickpea flour, for dredging

4 sprigs fresh thyme

1 10-ounce bag Dole® Italian Salad Mix

method

1. In a large sauté pan heat oil over medium-high heat.

2. Meanwhile, in a medium bowl combine fresh and smoked salmon, chickpeas, mayonnaise, and the 1 tablespoon lemon vinaigrette. Season with salt and pepper. Form into 4 patties, each about 1 inch thick. Dredge patties in chickpea flour. (See how-to photos, opposite.)

3. Add patties to oil and fry until golden brown and just cooked through, about 3 minutes per side. After you've turned patties over, top each one with a thyme sprig. Using a spoon, baste thyme with hot oil several times while patties finish cooking. Drain on paper towels, leaving thyme sprigs on top of patties.

4. Toss salad with remaining ¼ cup lemon vinaigrette; serve with salmon cakes.

the fix

It happens. Crab cakes and salmon patties sometimes crumble as they're being fried. If yours fall apart, it's far from a tragedy. Just toss the hot, crispy pieces of fish with the greens and dressing and eat them integrated with the salad rather than on top of it.

1. Spread the chickpea flour out onto a rimmed baking sheet or pizza pan. As you form each salmon patty, place it on the pan.

2. Dredge each patty in chickpea flour to coat, then gently pass it back and forth between your hands to get it to stick. Don't start frying until they've all been coated.

3. After you've turned the salmon patties over, top with thyme sprigs. Using a spoon, baste the sprigs a few times with hot oil —it infuses the salmon cakes with flavor.

SALMON FILLETS WITH TARRAGON BUTTER SAUCE & TREVISANO

If you like Belgian endive and radicchio, you'll love trevisano. It looks like endive that took a dip in a radicchio bath. It is a wonderful vegetable and makes a great salad green. **makes 4 servings**

grocery list

fresh

Four 6-ounce portions salmon fillet

3 large heads trevisano

packaged

⅔-ounce package fresh tarragon

12-ounce jar orange marmalade

staples

lemons

unsalted butter

vegetable oil

sherry vinegar

tools

small saucepan

large cast-iron skillet

ingredients

Juice of 2 lemons
2   tablespoons water
8   tablespoons unsalted butter
¼   cup chopped fresh tarragon
    Salt and freshly ground
    pepper
3   tablespoons vegetable oil
4   6-ounce portions salmon
    fillet
3   large heads trevisano or
    radicchio, roughly sliced,
    about 8 cups
3   tablespoons orange
    marmalade
1   tablespoon sherry vinegar

method

1. In a small saucepan, bring lemon juice and water to a boil over high heat. Whisk in butter, 2 tablespoons at a time, so that sauce is creamy and thickened (you can also use a handheld immersion blender to do this). Stir in tarragon and season to taste with salt and pepper. Remove from heat; cover to keep warm.
2. Meanwhile, in a large cast-iron skillet or large sauté pan heat 2 tablespoons of the oil over high heat. Season salmon with salt and pepper; cook until fish is just cooked through the center, about 3 minutes per side. Remove salmon from pan; cover lightly with foil to keep warm.
3. Add remaining tablespoon oil to pan. When oil is hot, add trevisano. Cook, stirring frequently, until trevisano is wilted and mostly tender, 4 to 5 minutes.
4. Season to taste with salt and pepper. Add marmalade and vinegar, stirring to combine.
5. Serve salmon with trevisano, spooning sauce over top of both.

the assist
If you can't find fresh tarragon, use one-quarter of the amount of dried. In this recipe, that would be 1 tablespoon.

SALMON IN TOMATO GRAVY WITH CUBANELLE PEPPERS & ONIONS

My family (and many Italian-Americans) call any tomato sauce made with meat "gravy." Even when there's no pasta present (and in this case, it's fish), it's still gravy to me. **makes 4 servings**

ingredients

2 tablespoons Bertolli® extra-virgin olive oil
2 large Cubanelle peppers, stemmed, seeded, and cut into large dice
1 large Vidalia onion, cut into large dice
   Salt and freshly ground pepper
1 35-ounce can whole peeled plum tomatoes, chopped, liquid reserved
1 12-ounce jar Heinz® pork gravy
⅓ cup Worcestershire sauce
1½ pounds salmon fillet, cut into 12 pieces, each about 1 inch thick and 1½ to 2 inches wide

method

1. In a large sauté pan, heat oil over medium heat. Add peppers and onion and cook, stirring occasionally, until tender, about 5 minutes. Season to taste with salt and pepper.
2. Add tomatoes and their liquid, gravy, and Worcestershire sauce; cover and bring to a simmer.
3. Season salmon with salt and pepper; add to the pan. Cover and simmer over low heat until fish is just cooked through, about 5 minutes. Season to taste with salt and pepper, if necessary, and serve.

grocery list

fresh

2 large Cubanelle peppers

1½ pounds salmon fillet

packaged

35-ounce can whole peeled plum tomatoes

12-ounce jar Heinz® pork gravy

staples

extra-virgin olive oil

Vidalia onion

Worcestershire sauce

tools

large sauté pan

SALMON EN CROÛTE WITH SPINACH & GRUYÈRE

I once helped cater a sit-down dinner for 2,000 at the Temple of Dendur in the Metropolitan Museum of Art. It was a fabulous setting with fabulous food. We served veal stuffed with spinach and Gruyère. Your surroundings may be more humble, but your dinner doesn't have to be. **makes 4 servings**

grocery list

fresh

Four 5-ounce portions skinless salmon fillet

packaged

3.15-ounce tube Amore® garlic paste

Two 10-ounce packages frozen chopped spinach

17.3-ounce package frozen puff pastry sheets

8-ounce package Gruyère cheese

staples

unsalted butter

yellow onion

flour

eggs

tools

large sauté pan

rimmed baking sheet

ingredients

2   tablespoons unsalted butter
1   small yellow onion, cut into small dice
2   tablespoons Amore® garlic paste, or 6 garlic cloves chopped
2   10-ounce packages frozen chopped spinach, thawed and squeezed dry
    Salt and freshly ground pepper
    Flour, for rolling pastry
1   sheet frozen puff pastry, thawed
4   5-ounce portions salmon skinless fillet, about 3½×3½ inches and 1 inch thick
8   1-ounce slices Gruyère cheese
1   egg
1   tablespoon water

method

1. Preheat oven to 425°F. In a large sauté pan over medium heat melt butter. Add onion and garlic paste and cook, stirring frequently, until onion is tender, about 4 minutes. Add spinach and cook, stirring occasionally, until liquid boils off, about 3 minutes. Season with salt and pepper. Cool slightly.

2. On a lightly floured surface roll pastry into a 9×18-inch rectangle. Cut rectangle in half lengthwise; cut each half in quarters to make 8 squares that each measure about 4½×4½ inches.

3. Line a rimmed baking sheet with parchment paper. Place 4 pastry squares on the parchment. Brush the edges of squares with water. Season salmon on both sides with salt and pepper. Lay 1 portion of salmon in the center of each pastry square. Top salmon with spinach mixture, dividing it equally among portions. Top the spinach with the cheese. Place remaining 4 pastry squares on top of the cheese. Using a fork, press the edges of the pastry to seal each salmon package. (For best results, refrigerate for 15 minutes.)

4. Whisk the egg with 1 tablespoon water; brush pastry with the egg wash. Bake until pastry is puffed and golden and salmon is cooked through, about 30 minutes.

SALMON WITH MUSTARD CRUST, TURNIP GREENS & BACON

Bacon, turnip greens, and onions are the holy trinity of Southern flavors. Slow-broiling the onions makes them sweet and soft, with a crunchy charred crust. **makes 4 servings**

ingredients

4   6-ounce portions skinless salmon fillet
Salt and freshly ground pepper
1   medium red onion, sliced very thin
⅓   cup Dijon mustard
⅓   pound thick-cut bacon, sliced into lardons (see how-to photos, page 73)
3   15-ounce cans turnip greens, drained

method

1. Preheat broiler on low. Line a rimmed baking sheet with foil. Season salmon with salt and pepper; lay on the prepared baking sheet.
2. Mix onions and mustard together. Divide evenly among the salmon portions, spreading to cover the surface of the fish completely. Broil until salmon is just cooked through and crust is lightly charred, about 8 minutes.
3. Meanwhile, in a large sauté pan cook bacon over medium heat. When bacon starts to turn golden but is not yet crispy, drain off all but 3 tablespoons fat. Add turnip greens to the pan and cook, stirring occasionally, until hot. Season to taste with salt and pepper; serve with salmon.

grocery list

fresh

Four 6-ounce portions skinless salmon fillet
⅓ pound thick-cut bacon

packaged

Three 15-ounce cans turnip greens

staples

red onion
Dijon mustard

tools

rimmed baking sheet

large sauté pan

TUNA AMANDINE WITH SNAP PEAS

"Amandine" is a serious throwback. All it means is that a dish has slivered almonds in it. So why not call it "almondine," you ask? It's one of those culinary Frenchifications that never got fully translated ("amande" is almond in French). **makes 4 servings**

ingredients

4   5-ounce tuna steaks
2   tablespoons Bertolli® extra-
    virgin olive oil
    Salt and freshly ground
    pepper
4   tablespoons unsalted butter
1   large Vidalia onion, sliced
    thin
12 ounces sugar snap peas
½   cup sliced almonds, toasted

method

1. Preheat broiler on high. Line a rimmed baking sheet with foil.
2. Coat tuna with olive oil; season generously with salt and pepper. Place on prepared baking sheet and broil about 2 minutes per side for rare.
3. Meanwhile, in a large cast-iron skillet or large sauté pan heat butter over high heat. When butter is golden brown, add onion and cook, stirring occasionally, until almost tender, about 8 minutes. Add snap peas; season to taste with salt and pepper. Cook, stirring occasionally, until snap peas are crisp-tender, about 4 more minutes.
4. Divide vegetables among 4 serving plates; top with tuna steaks. Sprinkle with almonds.

grocery list

fresh

Four 5-ounce tuna steaks

packaged

Two 8-ounce packages sugar snap peas

2.25-ounce package sliced almonds

staples

extra-virgin olive oil

unsalted butter

Vidalia onion

tools

rimmed baking sheet

large cast-iron skillet

the assist

Almonds burn easily. If you seem to be incinerating them in the oven, toast them on the stovetop in a skillet over medium heat. Shake and/or stir them occasionally to get them evenly toasted.

TUNA BURGERS WITH PEPPERONCINI & BASIL

Jennifer DelPesce (whose name means "with fish" in Italian) hated fish. Her husband loves it. Fish, in general, had become a sore subject in the DelPesce household. Jennifer was determined to learn how to cook fish—and I was determined to cure her hatred of it. **makes 2 servings**

ingredients

3 tablespoons butter
4 slices rye bread
½ cup mayonnaise
4 large pepperoncini
   (2 chopped, 2 left whole)
10 large basil leaves
   (6 chopped, 4 left whole)
2 tablespoons capers
10 ounces fresh tuna, diced
   Salt and freshly ground
   pepper
1 cup all-purpose flour, for
   dredging
2 eggs, lightly beaten
1 cup panko breadcrumbs
3 tablespoons vegetable oil
   Juice and zest of 1 lemon

method

1. In a large sauté pan, melt butter. Add rye bread and cook until bread is golden brown, turning to toast both sides.
2. In a medium bowl, combine the mayonnaise, chopped pepperoncini, chopped basil, and capers. Reserve half of the mayonnaise mixture and add tuna to the remaining half. Season the tuna mixture with salt and pepper; divide mixture in half; shape each half into a burger.
3. Dredge each burger in flour and then dip in the beaten eggs. Coat each burger thoroughly with panko breadcrumbs.
4. Wipe the sauté pan with a clean paper towel. Add the oil and heat over medium-high heat. When oil is hot, add tuna burgers and fry until golden brown but still slightly rare in center, about 2 minutes per side. Drain on paper towels.

5. Meanwhile, stir lemon juice and zest into the remaining mayonnaise mixture. Spread half on two slices of bread. Place tuna burgers on top of bread. Spread remaining mayonnaise on top of tuna. Place 2 basil leaves on top of tuna; top with remaining bread. Spear each whole pepperoncini with a toothpick and insert one into each sandwich to secure.

the fix

Instead of dredging the whole patties in flour, Jennifer tossed all of the diced tuna with flour—which, of course, meant that the patties wouldn't stay together. Each tiny piece of tuna was coated with flour—a perfect scenario for a fresh-tuna casserole. I found some frozen vegetables in the freezer, made a gravy, and took the rye bread meant for the sandwiches to make a buttery crumb topping. Who doesn't like creamy, bubbling tuna casserole?

SESAME TUNA NOODLES

Buttery, nutty-tasting sesame seeds have been adding flavor to food for more than 4,000 years. MIKEE® Sesame Teriyaki sauce is a great shortcut, but to really amp up the flavor of the classic combo of tuna and sesame, toss in some toasted sesame seeds before serving. **makes 4 servings**

ingredients

12 ounces egg noodles
3 tablespoons vegetable oil
1 pound fresh tuna, cut into bite-size chunks
Salt and freshly ground pepper
1 red onion, sliced thin
1 bunch scallions, greens only, sliced thin on a bias (see how-to photos, page 21)
1 mango, cut into large dice (see how-to photos, page 129)
2 cups MIKEE® Sesame Teriyaki Sauce
Pinch cayenne

method

1. Bring a stockpot of salted water to a boil. Cook egg noodles according to package directions, about 7 minutes.
2. Meanwhile, in a large cast-iron skillet or large sauté pan heat 2 tablespoons of the vegetable oil over high heat. Season tuna with salt and pepper; add to the pan. Cook, stirring occasionally, until brown on the outside but still rare on the inside, about 2 minutes. Remove tuna from pan; cover lightly with foil to keep warm.
3. Heat remaining tablespoon oil in pan. Add red onion and cook, stirring occasionally, until onion starts to get tender, about 5 minutes. Add scallions and continue to cook for another 2 minutes. Add mango and sesame sauce; bring to a simmer.
4. Toss tuna with noodles, sauce, and a pinch of cayenne to taste.

grocery list

fresh

1 pound fresh tuna

1 bunch scallions

1 mango

packaged

12-ounce package egg noodles

20-ounce MIKEE® Sesame Teriyaki Sauce

staples

vegetable oil

red onion

cayenne pepper

tools

stockpot

large cast-iron skillet

FRESH TUNA MELTS WITH CHEDDAR, SMOKED HAM & MANGO SALSA

I have been reinventing the tuna melt since I was a kid. This is its most recent incarnation. You might not think mango has a place in this great American classic, but oh boy, it is good! **makes 4 servings**

grocery list

fresh

1 small mango

4 slices smoked ham

12 ounces sushi-grade tuna

packaged

12-ounce jar hot salsa

1 loaf rye bread

8-ounce package white cheddar cheese

staples

mayonnaise

unsalted butter

tools

2 large sauté pans

ingredients

1   small mango, diced (see how-to photos, page 129)

½   cup hot salsa

8   slices rye bread

½   cup mayonnaise

8   slices white cheddar cheese

4   slices smoked ham

12 ounces sushi-grade tuna, sliced thin

Salt and freshly ground pepper

8   tablespoons unsalted butter

method

1. Heat two large sauté pans over medium heat.

2. Meanwhile, in a small bowl combine mango and salsa. Spread each slice of bread with 1 tablespoon mayonnaise. Lay 4 slices, mayo-side up, on a work surface. Top each piece of bread with one slice of cheese and one slice of ham. Divide the mango salsa among the four sandwiches.

3. Season the tuna with salt and pepper; lay on top of the salsa. Top the tuna with one more slice of cheese and the remaining slices of bread, mayo-side down.

4. Put 4 tablespoons of butter in each of the two sauté pans. When melted and hot, turn heat down to low; place 2 sandwiches in each pan. Cook until bread is deep golden brown, cheese is melted, and tuna is warm, about 4 minutes per side.

the assist

If you can't find sushi-grade tuna—and it's important that you use sushi-grade, as the tuna is only warmed and not cooked through—you can use smoked tuna, canned tuna, or even canned salmon.

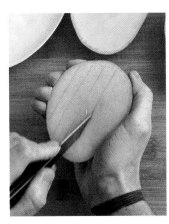

1. Make a cut through the mango, sliding the knife next to the seed along one side of the mango. Repeat on the other side of the seed, giving you two large pieces.

2. Work with one of the large pieces at a time. Make crosshatch cuts through the meat just to the peel, but not through the peel.

3. Bend the peel back and carefully slide the knife between the peel and the meat to remove the meat from the peel. Cut up any large pieces. Discard the peel.

SPICY **TUNA** ROLLS & MUSHROOM-ASPARAGUS ROLLS

Chip Thomas thought it was time his mother and his girlfriend's mother met. (Meeting over food is always a good idea.) Problem was, Chip's girlfriend and mom were vegetarians—he and his mom were not. A big tray of mixed sushi was the perfect solution—and singled no one out. **makes 4 servings**

ingredients

2   cups short-grain sushi rice
3   tablespoons sushi seasoning
8   sheets nori

For the Spicy Tuna
7½ ounces sushi-quality tuna, diced
2   to 3 tablespoons mayonnaise
1   tablespoon Sriracha
1   scallion, finely chopped
    Togarashi (spice blend)
    Salt

For Mushroom-Asparagus Rolls
4   spears asparagus, woody
    stems trimmed
2   tablespoons toasted sesame oil
1   clove garlic, chopped
1   tablespoon chopped fresh
    ginger
2   scallions, finely chopped
3   cups sliced shiitake
    mushroom caps
2   tablespoons soy sauce
1   tablespoon rice wine vinegar
1   tablespoon mirin
    Zest and juice of 1 lime

For serving
    Wasabi paste
    Pickled ginger
    Soy sauce

method

1. Cook rice in rice cooker according to package instructions. Spread cooked rice in a wide, shallow bowl; sprinkle with sushi seasoning. Cover with a clean towel and allow to cool.
2. For Spicy Tuna Roll: In a medium bowl combine tuna, mayonnaise, Sriracha, scallion, and togarashi and salt to taste. Mix thoroughly.
2. For Mushroom-Asparagus Roll: Bring a stockpot of salted water to a boil. Add asparagus and cook for 5 minutes; remove from pot and immediately plunge into a bowl of ice-cold water to stop the cooking process; set aside.
3. In a large sauté pan heat sesame oil over high heat. Add garlic, ginger, and scallions. Cook, stirring, until very fragrant, about 1 minute. Add mushrooms and cook until tender, about 5 minutes. Add soy sauce, rice wine vinegar, and mirin; remove from heat. Stir in lime juice and zest. Allow to cool.

4. To assemble sushi: Line a bamboo sushi mat with plastic wrap. Lay a sheet of nori on the mat. Spread a small amount of rice over the nori to cover it completely. Flip the nori over on the mat so the rice side is facing down. For the tuna roll, arrange a line of tuna mixture along one edge of the nori. Beginning at that edge, use the bamboo mat to roll and shape sushi. Slice and arrange on a serving platter. Repeat with 3 more sheets of nori.
5. For the vegetable roll, repeat process of spreading rice and flipping nori. Make a line of mushroom mixture along one edge of the nori. Lay one stalk of asparagus next to the mushroom mixture. Repeat rolling, shaping, and slicing.
6. Serve sushi with wasabi, pickled ginger, and soy sauce.

the fix

Chip hadn't thought of dessert—and something sweet is a nice way to end a meal when you're trying to make someone sweet on you. So I took leftover cooked rice and stirred in some raspberry yogurt his mom had in her refrigerator. With that, some diced mango, and black sesame seeds he had for the savory roll, I made a sushi dessert handroll.

TUNA & TOMATO CRUMBLE

Doesn't the word "crumble" conjure up delicious visions? I fell in love with crumble when I learned how to make Apple Brown Betty as a teenager apprenticing in Paris. This is a savory turn on that highly adaptable fruit dessert. **makes 4 servings**

ingredients

⅔ pound fresh tuna, cut into bite-size chunks
3 6-ounce cans oil-packed tuna, drained
1 pint grape tomatoes
2 14-ounce cans mustard greens, drained and squeezed of excess moisture
1 cup light mayonnaise
2 tablespoons Amore® garlic paste, or 6 garlic cloves, chopped
1 cup chopped fresh basil
Salt and freshly ground pepper
1 4-ounce package Parmesan crackers, preferably Eli Zabar® Toasted Parmesan Bread Crisps

method

1. Preheat oven to 350°F.
2. In a large bowl combine fresh tuna, canned tuna, tomatoes, mustard greens, mayonnaise, garlic paste, and basil. Season generously with salt and pepper. Spread mixture in a 9x13-inch glass baking dish. Crumble crackers on top.
3. Bake until bubbling, about 30 to 35 minutes. Let stand 5 minutes before serving.

grocery list

fresh
⅔ pound fresh tuna
1 pint grape tomatoes

packaged
Three 6-ounce cans oil-packed tuna
Two 14-ounce cans mustard greens
3.15-ounce tube Amore® garlic paste
1 bunch fresh basil
4-ounce package Eli Zabar® Toasted Parmesan Bread Crisps

staples
light mayonnaise

tools

9x13-inch glass baking dish

GRILLED **TUNA** NIÇOISE SALAD

Tuna is extremely lean, which is why it can be a little dry—that's why we add mayo to tuna salad. A lighter way to bring richness to tuna is with the addition of hardboiled eggs, as in this classic dish from Nice, in the south of France. **makes 4 servings**

grocery list

fresh

Four 5-ounce tuna steaks

packaged

8-ounce package sugar snap peas

15-ounce can sweet potatoes

2-ounce can anchovy fillets in oil

1-ounce package fresh basil

staples

eggs

extra-virgin olive oil

lemons

tools

small saucepan

large sauté pan

ingredients

4 eggs
4 5-ounce tuna steaks
¼ cup plus 3 tablespoons Bertolli® extra-virgin olive oil
   Salt and freshly ground pepper
8 ounces sugar snap peas
1 15-ounce can sweet potatoes, drained and cut into bite-size cubes
1 2-ounce can anchovy fillets in oil, drained and roughly chopped
   Juice and zest of 2 lemons
½ cup finely chopped fresh basil

method

1. Place eggs in a small saucepan and cover with water by 1 inch. Bring to a simmer over high heat, then turn off burner. Let eggs sit in water for about 10 minutes. Cool and peel. Cut crosswise into ¼-inch-thick slices; set aside.
2. Preheat grill/grill pan/broiler. (If using the broiler, line a rimmed baking sheet with foil.)
3. Coat tuna with 2 tablespoons of the olive oil; season generously with salt and pepper. Grill about 1½ minutes per side for rare. Let rest 5 minutes, then cut into ½-inch-thick slices.
4. Meanwhile, in a large sauté pan heat 1 tablespoon olive oil over medium heat. Add snap peas and cook, stirring, until they just start to get tender, about 2 minutes. Add sweet potatoes; season to taste with salt and pepper.
5. Make a bed of the vegetables on a serving platter; arrange tuna slices on top of vegetables. Top tuna with egg slices.
6. In a small bowl, combine anchovies, lemon juice and zest, basil, and remaining ¼ cup olive oil. Season to taste with salt and pepper, if necessary, and spoon generously over tuna salad.

CHARRED CHILEAN SEA **BASS** WITH MISO & MARMALADE

This was one of the dishes I developed for Jennifer DelPesce (see her story, page 126). I figured if I was going to change the mind of a fish hater, I'd better start with a mild, buttery, meaty fish like sea bass. Add a little savory (miso) and a little sweet (marmalade), and you're set. **makes 2 servings**

ingredients

½   cup white miso
½   cup orange marmalade
2   tablespoons Bertolli® extra-
     virgin olive oil
2   tablespoons chopped fresh
     tarragon
     Juice of 1 lemon
1   1-pound Chilean sea bass
     filet
     Salt and freshly ground
     black pepper

method

1. Preheat broiler on low. Line a rimmed baking sheet with foil.

2. In a medium bowl, combine miso, marmalade, olive oil, tarragon, and lemon juice. Place sea bass on prepared baking sheet: season with salt and pepper. Evenly coat the entire surface of the filet with the miso mixture. Broil for about 12 minutes. or until fish is charred and just cooked through. (Turn broiler heat up, if necessary, to achieve the desired charring.)

the fix

Miso and marmalade make a great glaze for fish—and although you want it to char a fair amount, half of the glaze on Jennifer's filet was almost sooty and the other half undercooked. (Her broiler must cook unevenly.) So I scraped off all of it, stirred it up and spread it out over the whole filet. Everybody's happy.

POPCORN **MONKFISH** WITH SPICY MAYO

I couldn't resist doing something playful with fish for Jennifer DelPesce (see page 134). Even if you're not a big fish fan, certainly little bits of it, crisp-fried and crunchy like popcorn and served with a spicy mayo, are going to prove irresistible. **makes 2 servings**

ingredients

1   quart vegetable oil
1   ½-pound monkfish filet, cut
     into 1-inch cubes
1   egg white, beaten
1   cup fine cornmeal
     Salt and freshly ground
     pepper
½   cup mayonnaise
2   tablespoons chili-garlic
     sauce
2   tablespoons Tabasco® Red
     Pepper Jelly
     Juice of 1 lime
⅓   cup chopped fresh cilantro

method

1. In a large pasta pot, heat oil to 375°F.
2. Meanwhile, in a medium bowl, coat monkfish in egg white. Drain and dredge in the cornmeal. Add to hot oil, stirring gently with a slotted skimmer to prevent the cubes from sticking and clumping. Fry until golden brown and just cooked through, about 3 minutes. Drain on a paper towel-lined plate; season with salt and pepper.

3. Meanwhile, in a medium bowl combine mayonnaise, chili-garlic sauce, jelly, and lime juice; whisk to thoroughly combine.
4. Add monkfish to bowl and toss with cilantro. Season to taste with salt and pepper and serve immediately.

the fix

When Jennifer coated her fish in egg white and then in cornmeal, the cornmeal didn't stick; it just slid right off. I just rinsed it all off with water—then patted it dry really well with paper towels (water and hot oil are a spatter-inducing combination), then coated it in egg white and cornmeal again. No harm, no foul.

> Nothing tastes as much of the sea as **SHELL-FISH.** Whether it's shrimp, crab, or lobster, every bite is one of perfect briny sweetness.

SHRIMP AU POIVRE WITH BROILED ZUCCHINI

This was a dish I tossed together in about 2 minutes when I was in a bad mood recently. I won't get into the details of my bad mood, but I will tell you that I ended up feeling very, very happy. **makes 4 servings**

grocery list

fresh

3 large zucchini

1¼ pounds raw shrimp

1 bunch scallions

packaged

10-ounce jar Tabasco®
Spicy Red Pepper Jelly

6-ounce can
pineapple juice

staples

extra-virgin olive oil

unsalted butter

tools

rimmed baking sheet

large sauté pan

ingredients

3   large zucchini, sliced in half
    horizontally and sliced into
    half moons
2   tablespoons Bertolli® extra-
    virgin olive oil
    Salt and freshly ground
    pepper
4   tablespoons unsalted butter
¼   cup fresh coarsely ground
    black pepper
1¼ pounds raw shrimp, peeled
    and deveined (see how-to
    photos, page 145)
1   bunch scallions, sliced
    thin on a bias (see how-to
    photos, page 21)
1   10-ounce jar Tabasco® Spicy
    Red Pepper Jelly
½   cup pineapple juice

method

1. Preheat broiler on high. Line a rimmed baking sheet with foil. Toss the zucchini with olive oil and salt and pepper to taste. Spread out in a single layer on the prepared baking sheet. Broil, stirring and turning occasionally, until lightly charred and tender, about 6 minutes.

2. Meanwhile, in a large sauté pan or cast-iron skillet, heat butter over medium heat. Season shrimp with salt and dredge one side in the coarsely ground black pepper. When butter is hot and foamy, add shrimp to the pan. Cook until just cooked through, about 2 minutes per side.

3. Remove shrimp from pan and add scallions. Cook, stirring occasionally, for about 2 minutes. Add red pepper jelly and pineapple juice and bring to a boil. Cook until sauce is slightly reduced, about 3 minutes.

4. Arrange shrimp on a bed of the broiled zucchini. Spoon pepper-pineapple sauce on top and serve.

BROILED **SHRIMP** WITH PARMIGIANO-GARLIC BREAD PUDDING

I served Shrimp Scampi at a great upstate New York resort when I was a student at the Culinary Institute of America. I've seen hundreds of variations, but this might be my favorite. **makes 4 servings**

grocery list

fresh

1½ pounds raw shrimp

packaged

1 loaf sourdough bread

Two 8-ounce cartons heavy cream

3.15-ounce tube Amore® garlic paste

staples

eggs

Parmigiano-Reggiano cheese

unsalted butter

lemons

tools

rimmed baking sheet

8x8-inch glass baking dish

ingredients

5 cups cubed sourdough bread
4 eggs
1¾ cups heavy cream
4 tablespoons Amore® garlic paste, or 12 garlic cloves, chopped
1 cup grated Parmigiano-Reggiano cheese
Salt and freshly ground pepper
6 tablespoons unsalted butter, melted, plus additional for baking dish
1½ pounds raw shrimp, peeled and deveined (see how-to photos, page 145)
Juice of 2 lemons

method

1. Preheat oven to 350°F.
2. Lay bread on a rimmed baking sheet. Toast in the oven until golden, 10 to 15 minutes, stirring occasionally. Cool.
3. In a large bowl, whisk together eggs, cream, 3 tablespoons of the garlic paste (or about three-fourths of the chopped garlic), and ⅔ cup of the cheese. Add toasted bread to the bowl and stir to combine. Season with salt and pepper.
4. Brush an 8×8-inch glass baking dish with enough butter to coat the bottom and sides. Pour the bread mixture into the dish and top with the remaining ⅓ cup cheese. Bake until pudding is set and golden brown, about 30 minutes.
5. Remove pudding from oven. Preheat broiler on high. Combine the 6 tablespoons melted butter with the remaining garlic. Toss the shrimp in the garlic butter and lay in a single layer on a rimmed, foil-lined baking sheet. Season generously with salt and pepper.
6. Broil until shrimp are just cooked through, about 3 minutes. Sprinkle with lemon juice. Spoon shrimp and lemon-garlic butter over the bread pudding and serve immediately.

MAC 'N' CHEESE WITH **SHRIMP**

I know, I know—mac 'n' cheese with shrimp, how could I? Well, I did it, and you're gonna love it, guaranteed. Make sure you season those breadcrumbs well and don't skimp on the butter. Let's face it: If you're serving this dish, you're indulging your id anyway. **makes 4 servings**

ingredients

1   18-ounce can Progresso® Creamy Mushroom Soup
2   tablespoons all-purpose flour
1   pound white cheddar cheese, shredded
1   pound elbow macaroni, cooked according to package directions
½   pound cooked ham steak, diced
1   pound raw shrimp, peeled and deveined (see how-to photos, page 145)
    Salt and freshly ground pepper
1½ cups panko breadcrumbs
½   cup melted butter

method

1. Preheat oven to 400°F.
2. In a medium saucepan bring soup to a boil. Sprinkle in flour, whisking as you add it. Boil the soup until thickened, about 3 minutes. Whisk in half of the cheese.
3. In a large bowl combine mushroom-cheese sauce with macaroni, ham, and shrimp. Season with salt and pepper.
4. Transfer macaroni mixture to a 9×13-inch baking dish. Top with remaining cheese. Toss the breadcrumbs with the melted butter; season to taste with salt and pepper. Sprinkle breadcrumbs over cheese. Bake until topping is golden brown and casserole is hot throughout, about 20 minutes.

grocery list

fresh

½ pound cooked
ham steak

1 pound raw shrimp

packaged

18-ounce can Progresso®
Creamy Mushroom Soup

16-ounce package white
cheddar cheese

1-pound package
elbow macaroni

7-ounce package panko
breadcrumbs

staples

flour

butter

tools

medium saucepan

9x13-inch baking dish

SHRIMP HASH & EGGS

My top choice for a New York City diner breakfast is corned beef hash with eggs. Hash is the ultimate forage-in-your-fridge dish. It can be made with just about any protein—leftover salmon, grilled pork chops, roasted chicken, steak—or shrimp. This would be great served over rice. **makes 4 servings**

grocery list

fresh

4 slices bacon

1 pound raw shrimp

packaged

Two 13.5-ounce cans diced potatoes

12-ounce jar Mancini® fried peppers

staples

extra-light olive oil

Cajun seasoning

white vinegar

eggs

tools

large sauté pan

medium saucepan

ingredients

3 tablespoons Bertolli® extra light olive oil

2 13.5-ounce cans diced potatoes, drained
Salt and freshly ground pepper

4 slices bacon, diced

1 pound raw shrimp, peeled and deveined (see how-to photos, page 145)

1 12-ounce jar Mancini® fried peppers

2 tablespoons Cajun seasoning

2 tablespoons white vinegar

8 eggs

method

1. In a large cast-iron skillet or sauté pan, heat oil over medium heat. Add potatoes and cook, stirring often, until golden brown, about 8 minutes. Season with salt and pepper; remove from pan and drain on a paper towel-lined plate.
2. Wipe out pan with a clean paper towel; return pan to heat and add bacon. Cook, stirring occasionally, until bacon just starts to turn golden, about 4 minutes. Season shrimp with salt and pepper; add to pan. Cook, stirring occasionally, for 2 minutes. Add peppers and Cajun seasoning. Cook, stirring occasionally, until mixture is hot throughout, about 2 more minutes. Return potatoes to the pan; stir gently to combine. Season with salt and pepper.
3. Meanwhile, in a stockpot bring 2 quarts of well-salted water and the vinegar to a boil. Turn off heat. Carefully crack 4 eggs into the water, spacing them apart. Poach eggs for 45 seconds to 1 minute, depending on desired doneness. Remove eggs from water with a slotted spoon. Gently blot them with a clean paper towel. Place 2 eggs on each of 2 serving plates. Repeat with remaining 4 eggs.
4. Spoon shrimp hash on top of eggs and serve.

SHRIMP PAELLA WITH CHORIZO

Big, burly scoutmaster Michael Marosy is a stay-at-home dad who cooks, but he's never very enthusiastic about it. He's kind of the king of cremation—he tends to burn stuff. He wanted to invite his fellow scoutmasters over for a party. I figured a one-pot meal that could be made over a campfire or at home would be perfect. Paella burns easily, so I used precooked rice. **makes 4 servings**

ingredients

1 7-ounce link Spanish chorizo, cut in half horizontally and sliced into half moons (see how-to photos, page 65)

2 tablespoons Amore® garlic paste, or 6 garlic cloves, chopped

1 large tomato, diced

1 14-ounce can low-sodium chicken broth

1 teaspoon saffron
 Salt and freshly ground pepper

2 8.8-ounce packages Uncle Ben's® Original Long-Grain Ready Rice®

1 cup frozen peas

1¼ pounds raw shrimp, peeled and deveined (see how-to photos, page 145)

method

1. In a large sauté pan heat chorizo over medium heat until fat is rendered, about 3 minutes. Add garlic and cook, stirring, until fragrant. Add tomato, chicken broth, and saffron; bring to a simmer.

2. Season generously with salt and pepper. Add rice and frozen peas; stir to combine. Cover and bring up to a simmer. Let cook for about 2 minutes.

3. Season shrimp with salt and pepper and lay on top of rice mixture. Cover and continue to cook until shrimp are just done, about 4 more minutes.

4. Season with salt and pepper, if necessary, and serve.

the fix

I added some chicken thighs to this dish to make it heartier, and—contrary to his usual M.O.—Michael actually undercooked them. I took them out of the paella, microwaved them, and rebuilt the paella. He also forgot to devein the shrimp. You can actually devein cooked shrimp—you just rip off the part in the back where the vein is and it comes right off.

SHRIMP & LOBSTER STEW WITH CORN & ZUCCHINI

If you're feeling a little insecure about your cooking, serve lobster—and if you're feeling really insecure, serve shrimp AND lobster. This is a luxurious, winning dish even if you feel all-thumbs in the kitchen.

makes 4 servings

ingredients

2 16-ounce containers Pacific® Roasted Red Pepper and Tomato Soup
1 cup frozen corn
2 medium zucchini, cut in half horizontally and sliced into thin half-moons
¾ pound shrimp, peeled and deveined (see how-to photos, below)
    Salt and freshly ground pepper
8 ounces raw lobster meat
½ cup chopped fresh basil

method

1. In a large sauté pan, bring soup to a simmer over medium heat. Add corn; cover and simmer for 2 minutes. Stir in zucchini. After about 1 minute, turn heat down low so soup is at a gentle simmer. **2.** Season shrimp generously with salt and pepper and add to the pan. Gently poach shrimp for about 2 minutes. Add lobster meat. When lobster and shrimp are cooked through, stir in basil. **3.** Season to taste with salt and pepper, if necessary.

grocery list

fresh

2 medium zucchini

8 ounces raw lobster meat

¾ pound raw shrimp

packaged

Two 16-ounce containers Pacific® Roasted Red Pepper and Tomato Soup

10-ounce package frozen corn

1-ounce package fresh basil

tools

large sauté pan

1. To peel shrimp, hold onto the tail firmly and open the shell lengthwise down the body. Starting at the head, gently pull the outer shell from the shrimp. Then hold the shrimp at the head end and gently pull on the tail to remove.

2. To devein shrimp, use a sharp knife to make a slit along the back of the shrimp. Then, using the tip of your knife, gently remove the black vein that runs the length of its back. Rinse the shrimp in cold water to clean; pat dry.

SHRIMP WITH GRITS & CHEESE

Shrimp, bacon, and creamy, cheesy grits. Enough said. **makes 4 servings**

grocery list

fresh

⅓ pound bacon

1½ pounds raw shrimp

packaged

1-ounce package fresh thyme leaves

3.15-ounce tube Amore® garlic paste

18.4-ounce box quick-cooking grits

8-ounce package sharp cheddar cheese

staples

milk

tools

rimmed baking sheet

medium saucepan

ingredients

⅓ pound bacon

1½ pounds raw shrimp, peeled and deveined (see how-to photos, page 145)
Salt and freshly ground pepper

¼ cup fresh thyme leaves

1 tablespoon Amore® garlic paste, or 3 garlic cloves, chopped

2 cups milk

¾ cup quick-cooking grits

1½ cups shredded sharp cheddar cheese

method

1. Preheat broiler on high.
2. Lay bacon slices in a single layer on a large microwaveable plate. Cook bacon in microwave on high until crisp, about 6 minutes. (If your microwave doesn't have a turntable, give the plate a quarter-turn halfway through the cooking time.) Crumble bacon and reserve bacon fat.
3. Line a rimmed baking sheet with foil. Put shrimp in a large bowl; season with salt and pepper and toss with thyme, garlic paste, and the reserved bacon fat. Lay shrimp in a single layer on the prepared baking sheet. Broil until shrimp are just cooked through, about 4 minutes.
4. Meanwhile, in a medium saucepan bring milk to a boil over high heat. Whisk in grits. Turn heat down to low and cook according to package directions, about 4 minutes. When done, whisk in cheddar cheese. Season to taste with salt and pepper. Pour grits into a serving dish and sprinkle with crumbled bacon. Top with shrimp and serve.

WARM **SHRIMP** & POTATO SALAD WITH BACON

Sweet, vinegary German potato salad is usually served warm and flavored with bits of smoky bacon. My mom learned how to make a version of it when she worked in a German deli while I was in high school. I've added shrimp to a side dish to make a main dish. **makes 4 servings**

ingredients

1½ pounds Red Bliss potatoes
    Salt and freshly ground
    pepper
½ pound thick-cut bacon, diced
1¼ pounds raw shrimp, peeled
    and deveined (see how-to
    photos, page 145)
¼ cup sherry vinegar
½ cup Tabasco® Spicy Red
    Pepper Jelly
½ cup chopped fresh flat-leaf
    parsley

method

1. Put potatoes in a large saucepan and cover with cold water. Season water generously with salt; bring potatoes to a boil over high heat. Turn heat down to low and simmer until potatoes are tender, about 20 minutes. Drain and let cool slightly.

2. Meanwhile, in a large sauté pan cook bacon over medium heat, stirring occasionally, until golden brown and crispy, 6 to 7 minutes. Remove bacon from the pan; set it aside to drain on a paper towel-lined plate.

3. Season shrimp with salt and pepper. Turn heat under pan down to low and add shrimp to the bacon fat in the pan. Cook, stirring occasionally, until just cooked through, about 3 minutes. Add vinegar to the pan, stirring and scraping pan with a wooden spoon to loosen any flavorful browned bits. Add pepper jelly and allow to melt.

4. When potatoes are cool enough to handle but still very warm, cut them into ½-inch-thick slices and put in a large bowl.

5. Toss potatoes with shrimp mixture, crispy bacon, and parsley. Season to taste with salt and pepper and serve immediately.

see how-to photos, page 145

grocery list

fresh

1½ pounds Red Bliss
potatoes
½ pound thick-cut bacon
1¼ pounds raw shrimp
1 bunch flat-leaf parsley

packaged

10-ounce jar Tabasco®
Spicy Red Pepper Jelly

staples

sherry vinegar

tools

large saucepan

large sauté pan

SHRIMP & WHOLE WHEAT PASTA WITH BROCCOLI & WHITE BEANS

Leave the shrimp tails on if you think they look pretty. I usually cut them off before cooking to make them easier to eat—especially when they're mixed into a dish, as they are here. **makes 4 servings**

grocery list

fresh
1 head broccoli
1¼ pounds raw shrimp

packaged
1-pound package whole wheat spaghetti
24-ounce jar Bertolli® Vineyard Marinara with Burgundy
13.5-ounce can cannellini beans
1-ounce package fresh basil

staples
crushed red pepper
extra-virgin olive oil

tools

stockpot

large sauté pan

ingredients

¾ pound whole wheat spaghetti
1 medium head broccoli, cut into florets
1 24-ounce jar Bertolli® Vineyard Marinara with Burgundy
1 teaspoon crushed red pepper
1 13.5-ounce can cannellini beans, rinsed and drained
1¼ pounds raw shrimp, peeled and deveined (see how-to photos, page 145)
Salt and freshly ground pepper
½ cup chopped fresh basil
Bertolli® extra-virgin olive oil, for drizzling

method

1. Bring a large stockpot of salted water to a boil. Cook pasta according to package directions, about 11 minutes. Add broccoli florets to pasta water during last 3 minutes of cooking; drain.
2. Meanwhile, in a large sauté pan heat marinara, crushed red pepper, and beans over medium heat until simmering. Season shrimp with salt and pepper and add to sauce. Cover and cook until shrimp are just done, about 3 minutes.
3. Stir in basil. Toss shrimp mixture with pasta and broccoli. Season to taste with salt and pepper. Drizzle with olive oil and serve.

SCALLOPS WITH RED BEANS & RICE

When you're scallop shopping, steer clear of "wet" scallops. They're treated with a solution that makes browning or caramelizing them almost impossible. I feel so strongly about this that I'm gonna say it's better to buy frozen "dry" scallops than fresh "wet" ones. ***makes 4 servings***

ingredients

2   8.8-ounce packages Uncle Ben's® Vegetable Harvest Ready Whole Grain Medley™

1   15-ounce can red beans, rinsed and drained

3   tablespoons vegetable oil

1½ pounds large sea scallops
    Salt and freshly ground pepper

1   15-ounce container fresh salsa

1   envelope Goya Sazón® seasoning
    Juice of 1 lime

method

1. In a medium microwaveable bowl combine rice and beans; cover with plastic wrap and microwave on high until hot, about 4 minutes.

2. Meanwhile, in a large sauté pan heat oil over high heat. Pat scallops dry with a paper towel; season with salt and pepper. Cook until golden brown and just cooked through, about 2 minutes per side. Remove scallops from pan; cover lightly with foil to keep warm.

3. Wipe out pan with a clean paper towel. Add salsa, Sazón seasoning, and lime juice. Cook, stirring occasionally, until warm, 2 to 3 minutes. Season to taste with salt and pepper, if necessary.

4. Serve scallops on a bed of rice and beans; spoon salsa mixture on top.

grocery list

fresh

1½ pounds large
sea scallops

15-ounce container fresh
salsa

packaged

Two 8.8-ounce packages
Uncle Ben's® Vegetable
Harvest Ready Whole
Grain Medley™

15-ounce can red beans

6.3-ounce box Goya
Sazón® seasoning

staples

vegetable oil

lime

tools

microwaveable bowl

large sauté pan

HOT **CRAB** LOUIS SALAD

So who was Louis? I'm not sure anyone knows for sure, but we owe him serious gratitude for this dish. I took a little liberty with the classic and turned it into great brunch food, inspired by a Singaporean dish I fell in love with on a visit there. **makes 4 servings**

grocery list

fresh

1 pound king crabmeat

packaged

12-ounce package English muffins

8-ounce jar chili-garlic sauce

staples

red onion

lemons

unsalted butter

eggs

tools

grill pan

small saucepan

ingredients

1   large red onion, cut into
    ⅓-inch-thick slices
    Salt and freshly ground
    pepper
4   English muffins
    Juice and zest of 2 lemons
8   tablespoons unsalted butter,
    at room temperature
4   tablespoons cold unsalted
    butter
1   tablespoon chili-garlic
    sauce
1   pound king crabmeat
8   eggs, lightly beaten

method

1. Heat grill/grill pan/broiler over high heat. Season onions with salt and pepper and grill until lightly charred and tender, about 4 minutes per side. Cover loosely with foil to keep warm.
2. Toast English muffins to desired doneness. Cover lightly with foil to keep warm.
3. In a small saucepan, bring lemon juice and zest to a boil. Whisk in the 8 tablespoons butter and bring to a boil. Using a handheld immersion blender or a whisk, beat in 2 tablespoons of the cold butter until sauce is creamy, thickened, and smooth. Stir in chili-garlic sauce; season to taste with salt and pepper. Remove from heat; cover to keep warm.
4. In a large sauté pan, melt the remaining 2 tablespoons cold butter over medium heat. Add crabmeat and cook, stirring gently once or twice, just until warm, about 2 minutes. Season to taste with salt and pepper.
5. Season beaten eggs with salt and pepper; add to pan. Cook, stirring constantly, until eggs are just set but still slightly wet.
6. To serve, top English muffins with grilled onions. Spoon egg-crab mixture on top of onions. Spoon chili-lemon sauce over the top and serve.

CLAM & CORN CHOWDER WITH POTATOES & BACON

OK, so this is a dish where I cheat like crazy. This great corn soup makes it so easy.
Why do the work if someone already did it for you, and did it masterfully? **makes 4 servings**

ingredients

½ pound thick-cut bacon, cut into lardons (see how-to photos, page 73)

1 large Idaho potato, peeled and cut into small dice

1 10-ounce package frozen corn
    Salt and freshly ground pepper

1 teaspoon crushed red pepper

2 16-ounce containers Imagine® Organic Creamy Sweet Corn Soup

4 dozen littleneck clams

⅓ cup chopped fresh chives

method

1. In a Dutch oven, heat bacon over medium heat. When fat has rendered and bacon is just beginning to brown, add diced potato. Cook, stirring often, until potatoes are almost tender, about 5 minutes.

2. Add corn. Season to taste with salt and pepper and cook, stirring occasionally, until hot throughout, another 3 minutes. Add crushed red pepper and soup to the pan. Cover and bring to a simmer. Simmer until potatoes are tender, about 5 minutes.

3. Add clams to the pan. Cover and simmer until clams have just opened, about 5 minutes. (Discard any clams that don't open.) Stir in chives and season to taste with salt and pepper, if necessary.

grocery list

fresh

½ pound thick-cut bacon

1 large Idaho potato

4 dozen littleneck clams

1 bunch chives

packaged

10-ounce package frozen corn

Two 16-ounce containers Imagine® Organic Creamy Sweet Corn Soup

staples

crushed red pepper

tools

Dutch oven

MUSSEL & LENTIL STEW WITH CAPONATA & PEPPERONI

Here's a paradigm shift: Pepperoni is for more than pizza. It adds great, spicy flavor to these briny mussels. They're one of the least expensive seafood ingredients out there—and one of the most beautiful and perfect. **makes 4 servings**

grocery list

fresh

7.5-ounce link pepperoni

2 pounds mussels

packaged

24-ounce jar Bertolli®
Vineyard Marinara
with Burgundy

7.5-ounce jar Paesana™
caponata

20-ounce can Progresso®
Lentil Soup

1 bunch
fresh basil

staples

extra-virgin olive oil

tools

Dutch oven

ingredients

2 tablespoons Bertolli® extra-
    virgin olive oil

1 7.5-ounce link pepperoni,
    diced

1 24-ounce jar Bertolli®
    Vineyard Marinara with
    Burgundy

1 7.5-ounce jar caponata

1 20-ounce can Progresso®
    Lentil Soup

2 pounds mussels

1 cup chopped fresh basil
    Salt and freshly ground
    pepper

method

1. In a Dutch oven, heat olive oil over medium heat. When hot, add pepperoni and cook, stirring occasionally, until pepperoni begins to render its fat and turn slightly golden, about 3 minutes.
2. Add marinara sauce, caponata, and lentil soup. Bring to a simmer. Add mussels to the pot. Cover and simmer until mussels open, about 3 minutes. (Discard any mussels that don't open.)
3. Stir in basil and season to taste with salt and pepper.

" I've probably eaten more Italian Mama-homemade **PASTA** than most, but I never tire of it. Pick a shape, toss it with things you love, and dinner is on. **"**

MAMA'S MEATBALLS & **SPAGHETTI**

Wherever I go, this is my most-requested recipe. Taste it and you'll see why. **makes 6 servings**

grocery list

fresh

1 bunch flat-leaf parsley
½ pound ground beef
½ pound ground pork
½ pound ground veal

packaged

Two 28-ounce cans tomato puree

28-ounce can crushed tomatoes

6-ounce can tomato paste

14.5-ounce can chicken broth

1-pound package dried spaghetti

staples

garlic/onions

extra-virgin olive oil

crushed red pepper

sugar

plain dry breadcrumbs

eggs

Parmigiano-Reggiano cheese

tools

large saucepan

ingredients

for the marinara

3   cloves garlic, crushed
½   yellow onion, peeled and finely chopped
3   tablespoons Bertolli® extra-virgin olive oil
    Crushed red pepper
2   28-ounce cans tomato puree
1   28-ounce can crushed tomatoes
1   tablespoon tomato paste
1   cup chicken broth
1   teaspoon sugar
    Salt

for meatballs and spaghetti

⅓   cup chicken broth
¼   yellow onion
1   clove garlic, peeled
½   cup torn flat-leaf parsley
½   pound ground beef
½   pound ground pork
½   pound ground veal
⅓   plain dry breadcrumbs
2   eggs, lightly beaten
¼   cup freshly grated Parmigiano-Reggiano cheese, plus more for serving
1   teaspoon crushed red pepper
1   teaspoon salt
    Bertolli® extra-virgin olive oil
6   cups Mama's Marinara, or your favorite marinara
1   pound dried spaghetti

method

1. In a large saucepan cook the garlic and onion in olive oil over medium-low heat until garlic is tender and onions are translucent but not brown, about 10 minutes. Add crushed red pepper to taste.
2. Add tomato products. Pour chicken broth into one of the 28-ounce cans. Fill the rest of the way with water. Add to pan, along with sugar. Stir and bring to a simmer. Season with salt to taste; cover and simmer for 1 hour.
4. Meanwhile, make the meatballs: In a food processor puree chicken broth, onion, garlic, and parsley.
5. In a large bowl combine broth mixture, meat, breadcrumbs, eggs, cheese, crushed red pepper, and salt. Using your hands, gently combine; don't overmix.
6. Rub a little olive oil on your hands; form mixture into balls that are slightly larger than golf balls.
7. Pour about ½ inch olive oil into a large sauté pan. Heat over medium-high. When oil is hot, brown meatballs in batches.
8. As meatballs finish browning, lift them gently with a slotted spoon and add to marinara; cover and simmer for about 1 hour.
9. Cook spaghetti according to package directions. Serve meatballs and marinara over spaghetti, topped with additional Parmigiano-Reggiano, if desired.

LINGUINE WITH SHRIMP, OLIVES & PEPPERONCINI

I love the convenience of garlic paste—especially in a recipe like this one, where there's so much garlic to love. If you can't find garlic paste, you'll just have to do a little chopping. **makes 4 servings**

ingredients

1   1-pound package dried linguine
½   cup Bertolli® extra-virgin olive oil
¼   cup Amore® garlic paste, or 12 garlic cloves, chopped
2   cups Bertolli® Vineyard Marinara with Burgundy
1   pound raw shrimp, peeled and deveined (see how-to photos, page 145)
     Salt and freshly ground pepper
¾   cup pitted kalamata olives, chopped
¼   cup pepperoncini, chopped
⅔   cup chopped fresh flat-leaf parsley

method

1. In a large saucepan, cook linguine according to package directions, about 11 minutes.
2. Meanwhile, in a large sauté pan heat olive oil over medium heat. Add garlic paste and cook, stirring often, until fragrant and slightly golden, about 2 minutes.
3. Add the marinara sauce to the pan and bring to a simmer. Season the shrimp with salt and pepper; add to the pan. Stir to coat in sauce; cover pan. Cook until shrimp are just done, about 3 minutes. Add olives, pepperoncini, and parsley.
4. When linguine is done, drain and toss in sauce; season to taste with salt and pepper, if necessary.

grocery list

fresh

1 pound raw shrimp

1 bunch flat-leaf parsley

packaged

1-pound package dried linguine

3.15-ounce tube Amore® garlic paste

24-ounce jar Bertolli® Vineyard Marinara with Burgundy

12-ounce jar pitted kalamata olives

12-ounce jar pepperoncini

staples

extra-virgin olive oil

tools

large saucepan

large sauté pan

LINGUINE WITH CLAMS & BACON

I use pork and pork products just about every time I can get away with it, but there's something unique to the clam/bacon combo that's celebrated in many dishes from New England. The sweet sea flavor of the clams against the smoky bacon cuts a path like few combos. **makes 4 servings**

grocery list

fresh
½ pound thick-cut bacon

3 dozen littleneck clams

1 bunch flat-leaf parsley

packaged
1-pound package dried linguine

3.15-ounce tube Amore® garlic paste

staples
crushed red pepper

dry white wine

tools

stockpot

Dutch oven

ingredients

1   1-pound package dried linguine
    Salt and freshly ground pepper
½   pound thick-cut bacon, cut into lardons (see how-to photos, page 73)
¼   cup Amore® garlic paste, or 12 garlic cloves, chopped
1   teaspoon crushed red pepper
1½ cups dry white wine
3   dozen littleneck clams
1   cup chopped fresh flat-leaf parsley

method

1. Cook linguine in a stockpot of boiling salted water according to package directions.
2. Meanwhile, in a Dutch oven cook bacon over medium heat until it begins to brown. Add garlic paste; stir to break up. Cook until garlic is pale golden. Add crushed red pepper and wine. Let simmer until reduced by half, about 6 minutes.
3. Add clams. Cover and simmer just until clams open, about 5 minutes. (Discard any clams that don't open.)
4. Add parsley and drained linguine; toss to combine. Season to taste with salt and pepper, if necessary, and serve.

the fix
Pasta that comes in long strands—like spaghetti or linguine—can sometimes stick together in clumps as it cooks. (Frequent stirring with a fork can prevent this). If this happens, just drain it, rinse it with some cool water, and pull the clumps out by hand. You can use the rest.

LINGUINE WITH OLIVES & FRESH MOZZARELLA

Who has time to pit olives? That's why I use olive paste (aka tapenade) whenever I want that rich, round olive flavor without messing around with the pits. **makes 4 servings**

ingredients

1   1-pound package dried linguine
    Salt and freshly ground pepper
1   cup Bertolli® extra-virgin olive oil
2   tablespoons Amore® garlic paste, or 6 garlic cloves, chopped
1½ cups coarsely crumbled stale French or Italian bread
⅔   cup olive paste
1   teaspoon crushed red pepper
1   pound fresh mozzarella, cut into ½-inch chunks
¾   cup chopped fresh flat-leaf parsley

method

1. Cook linguine in a stockpot of boiling salted water according to package directions.
2. In a large sauté pan, heat ½ cup of the olive oil over medium-low heat. Add garlic paste and stir to break up. Add breadcrumbs and cook, stirring often, until golden brown, about 5 minutes. Remove breadcrumbs from the pan; set aside.
3. Wipe out the pan with a clean paper towel and return to the heat. Add the remaining ½ cup olive oil and olive paste to the pan and cook, stirring occasionally, just until warm, about 3 to 4 minutes.
4. In a large bowl combine hot drained pasta, olive paste mixture, crushed red pepper, mozzarella, and parsley. Season to taste with salt and pepper and toss to thoroughly combine.
5. Top with breadcrumbs; serve.

grocery list

fresh
1 pound fresh mozzarella
1 bunch flat-leaf parsley

packaged
1-pound package dried linguine
3.15-ounce tube Amore® garlic paste
1 loaf French or Italian bread
4.5-ounce jar olive paste

staples
extra-virgin olive oil
crushed red pepper

tools

stockpot

large sauté pan

SPAGHETTI TONNATO

I call for oil-packed tuna here (vs. water-packed) because I think it has a richer, meatier flavor. Yes, it has a few more calories, but the flavor is worth the indiscretion. More specifically, look for the stuff packed in olive oil (vs. vegetable oil). **makes 4 servings**

grocery list

fresh

2 Cubanelle peppers

packaged

1-pound package dried spaghetti

3.15-ounce tube Amore® garlic paste

Two 6-ounce cans oil-packed tuna

3½-ounce jar capers

1 bunch fresh basil

staples

extra-virgin olive oil

crushed red pepper

ingredients

1 pound dried spaghetti
  Salt and freshly ground pepper
½ cup Bertolli® extra-virgin olive oil
2 tablespoons Amore® garlic paste, or 6 garlic cloves, chopped
2 Cubanelle peppers, seeded and sliced thin
½ teaspoon crushed red pepper
2 6-ounce cans oil-packed tuna
¼ cup capers
¾ cup chopped fresh basil

method

1. Cook spaghetti in a stockpot of boiling salted water according to package directions.

2. In a large sauté pan heat olive oil over medium heat. Add garlic paste and stir to break up. Add peppers and season to taste with salt and pepper. Cook, stirring occasionally, until tender, about 5 minutes.

3. Add crushed red pepper, tuna, and capers. Cook, stirring occasionally, until tuna is warm, about 3 minutes.

4. In a large bowl, toss drained spaghetti with pepper-tuna mixture and basil. Season to taste with salt and pepper and serve.

tools

stockpot

large sauté pan

ROASTED SPAGHETTI SQUASH WITH KALE & **LASAGNA**

This combination features two kinds of "pasta." There's the filled, layered and baked lasagna—and the toothsome, nutty-tasting strands of baked spaghetti squash. **makes 4 servings**

ingredients

½ 3-pound spaghetti squash

¼ cup Bertolli® extra-virgin olive oil

2 24-ounce packages Bertolli® Oven Bake Meals® Meat Rustica Lasagna

¾ teaspoon crushed red pepper

2 tablespoons Amore® garlic paste, or 4 garlic cloves, chopped

⅓ cup low-sodium chicken broth

1 10-ounce package Cut 'N Clean Rainbow Kale
  Salt and freshly ground pepper

method

1. Preheat oven to 400°F.

2. Using a large spoon, scrape the seeds and excess fibers out of the spaghetti squash half.

3. Line a rimmed baking sheet with aluminum foil. Brush the cut side of the squash with a little of the olive oil and place, cut side down, on the baking sheet. Cover tightly with foil. Put the squash and the lasagna in the oven at the same time and cook lasagna according to package directions.

4. Roast the squash for 15 minutes. While squash is cooking, combine remaining olive oil, crushed red pepper, garlic paste, and chicken broth in a large bowl. Add kale and toss thoroughly to combine. Season with salt and pepper and toss again.

4. Remove squash from the oven and unwrap. Pile kale mixture on the pan around the squash. Cover tightly with foil and return to the oven. Continue to roast another 35 minutes or until squash and kale are tender.

4. Using a large spoon, scrape the flesh out of the squash shell onto the pan. Toss with the kale. Season to taste with salt and pepper and serve with the lasagna.

grocery list

fresh

3-pound spaghetti squash

packaged

Two 24-ounce packages Bertolli® Oven Bake Meals® Meat Rustica Lasagna

3.15-ounce tube Amore® garlic paste

10-ounce package Cut 'N Clean Rainbow Kale

staples

extra-virgin olive oil

crushed red pepper

low-sodium chicken broth

tools

rimmed baking sheet

FETTUCCINE WITH RIBBONS OF ROAST BEEF, ARTICHOKES & BOURSIN

Creamy, spreadable Boursin cheese and artichokes are a great hors d'oeuvre—and a great way to add flavor and texture to a yummy pasta dish. The roast beef makes it a real meal. **makes 4 servings**

ingredients

¾ pound dried fettuccine
    Salt and freshly ground
    pepper
½ cup Bertolli® extra-virgin
    olive oil
2 tablespoons Amore®
    garlic paste, or 6 garlic
    cloves, chopped
1 14-ounce can quartered
    artichoke hearts, drained
1 12-ounce jar roasted red
    pepper strips, preferably
    Paesana™ Fire Roasted
    Peppers in Garlic & Extra-
    Virgin Olive Oil, drained
1 pound sliced rare roast
    beef, cut into ¼-inch-thick
    ribbons
2 5.2-ounce packages Boursin®
    Garlic & Fine Herbs cheese
½ cup chopped fresh basil

method

1. Cook fettuccine in a stockpot of boiling salted water according to package directions.
2. Meanwhile, in a large sauté pan heat olive oil over medium heat. Add garlic paste, stirring to break up. Cook and stir for about 1 minute. Add artichoke hearts and roasted red peppers. When vegetables are hot, after about 3 minutes, stir in roast beef and continue to cook, stirring gently, just until beef is warm, about another 2 minutes.
3. In a large bowl, combine fettuccine, beef mixture, cheese, and basil. Toss well to combine. Season to taste with salt and pepper.

grocery list

fresh

1 pound sliced
rare roast beef

packaged

1-pound package dried
fettuccine

3.15-ounce tube Amore®
garlic paste

14-ounce can quartered
artichoke hearts

12-ounce jar Paesana™
Fire Roasted Peppers
in Garlic & Extra-Virgin
Olive Oil

Two 5.2-ounce packages
Boursin® Garlic & Fine
Herbs cheese

1-ounce package fresh
basil

staples

extra-virgin olive oil

tools

large sauté pan

RIGATONI WITH TOMATOES, RICOTTA & WALNUTS

Rigatoni is one of the biggest, baddest, toothiest pastas, so it needs to be served with a hearty, big-flavored sauce substantial enough to stand up to it. The ricotta-and-walnut combination in this recipe makes a perfect match. **makes 4 servings**

grocery list

fresh

1 bunch flat-leaf parsley

packaged

1-pound package dried rigatoni

24-ounce jar Bertolli® Vineyard Marinara with Burgundy

15-ounce container whole milk ricotta

8-ounce bag chopped walnuts

staples

extra-virgin olive oil

Parmigiano-Reggiano cheese

tools

stockpot

large microwaveable bowl

ingredients

1   pound dried rigatoni
    Salt and freshly ground
    pepper
1   24-ounce jar Bertolli®
    Vineyard Marinara with
    Burgundy
1   pound whole-milk ricotta
1½ cups walnuts, toasted and
    finely chopped
⅓   cup Bertolli® extra-virgin
    olive oil
1   cup chopped fresh flat-leaf
    parsley
1   cup grated Parmigiano-
    Reggiano cheese

method

1. Cook rigatoni in a stockpot of boiling salted water according to package directions.
2. Empty pasta sauce into a large microwaveable bowl and cover with plastic wrap. Microwave on high until hot, about 3 minutes.
3. Add cooked rigatoni, ricotta, walnuts, olive oil, parsley, and Parmigiano-Reggiano. Season to taste with salt and pepper; toss to combine and serve.

ORECCHIETTE WITH SHRIMP, TOMATO & SARDINES

Sardines are nutritional powerhouses that are thought to do everything from prevent cancer to make you smarter. They are also, pound for pound, one of the most flavorful little fish to come out of the ocean. Start with a small amount, if you're tentative. You won't be for long. **makes 4 servings**

ingredients

1   pound dried orecchiette
    Salt and freshly ground
    pepper
½   cup Bertolli® extra-virgin
    olive oil
1   3.15-ounce tube Amore®
    garlic paste, or 10 garlic
    cloves, chopped
2   cups canned peeled plum
    tomatoes, drained and
    roughly chopped
2   cups Bertolli® Premium
    Summer Crushed Tomato &
    Basil pasta sauce
1   pound raw shrimp, peeled,
    deveined, and split in half
    (see how-to photos,
    page 145)
½   cup chopped fresh basil
1   3.75-ounce can Bumble Bee®
    sardines, chopped fine

method

1. Cook orecchiette in a stockpot of boiling salted water according to package directions.
2. Meanwhile, in a large sauté pan heat olive oil over medium heat. Add the garlic paste and cook, stirring to break up, until golden brown, about 6 minutes. Add tomatoes and pasta sauce and bring to a simmer.
3. Season shrimp with salt and pepper and add to the sauce. Stir to coat and cook until shrimp are just done, about 2 minutes.
4. Stir in basil and sardines. Toss pasta with shrimp-tomato mixture. Season to taste with salt and pepper and serve.

grocery list

fresh

1 pound raw shrimp

packaged

1-pound package dried orecchiette

3.15-ounce tube Amore® garlic paste

28-ounce can peeled plum tomatoes

Two 13.5-ounce pouches Bertolli® Premium Summer Crushed Tomato & Basil pasta sauce

1-ounce package fresh basil

3.75-ounce can Bumble Bee® sardines

staples

extra-virgin olive oil

tools

large sauté pan

PERCIATELLI & OCTOPUS AMATRICIANA

Garlicky octopus lends a touch of exotica to this dish. Although "amatriciana" (translation: contains hot peppers) is generally made with bucatini, perciatelli is essentially the same thing—a hollow spaghetti-like pasta tube that's thicker than spaghetti. **makes 4 servings**

grocery list

fresh

½ pound thick-cut bacon

1 bunch flat-leaf parsley

packaged

1-pound package dried perciatelli

Two 13.5-ounce pouches Bertolli® Premium Summer Crushed Tomato & Basil pasta sauce

8.5-ounce jar sliced hot cherry peppers

Five 4-ounce packages Bajamar Octopus in Garlic Sauce

staples

onion

tools

stockpot

large sauté pan

ingredients

1 pound dried perciatelli
½ pound thick-cut bacon, cut into 1-inch pieces
1 large yellow onion, cut into small dice
2 13.5-ounce pouches Bertolli® Premium Summer Crushed Tomato & Basil pasta sauce (about 3 cups)
¼ cup sliced hot cherry peppers
    Salt and freshly ground pepper
5 4-ounce packages octopus, preferably Bajamar Octopus in Garlic Sauce
⅓ cup chopped fresh flat-leaf parsley

method

1. Cook perciatelli in a stockpot of boiling salted water according to package directions.

2. In a large sauté pan, cook bacon over medium heat until fat begins to render, about 2 to 3 minutes. When bacon begins to brown, add onion. Cook, stirring occasionally, until onion is tender, about 5 minutes. Add pasta sauce and cherry peppers; season to taste with salt and pepper.

3. Bring mixture to a simmer; add octopus. Cover and simmer just until octopus is warmed through, about 2 minutes. Add cooked pasta and parsley to the pan; toss to coat. Season to taste with salt and pepper, if necessary.

the assist

Admittedly, not every corner store carries canned octopus. If the one you frequent doesn't happen to, you can use canned crab, oysters, or mussels—all will work and taste just fine in this recipe.

SPINACH & BOURSIN **RAVIOLI**

Rob Capobianco wanted to surprise his girlfriend (see his story, page 26) and make her a very memorable meal. He knew she loved fresh pasta, but he was intimidated by the prospect of making it. So we made fresh ravioli with already-made dough—wonton wrappers. **makes 2 servings**

ingredients

4   ounces frozen spinach, thawed
½   small yellow onion, cut into fine dice
3   ounces Boursin® Garlic & Fine Herbs cheese
3   ounces Boursin® Shallot & Chive cheese
3   ounces Boursin® Pepper cheese
    Salt and freshly ground pepper
1   egg, beaten
1   tablespoon water
24 wonton skins
    All-purpose flour
1   cup heavy cream
1½ cups Bertolli® Summer Crushed Tomato & Basil pasta sauce
¼   cup vodka
3   tablespoons sliced fresh basil
    Bertolli® extra-virgin olive oil, for drizzling
    Freshly grated Parmigiano-Reggiano cheese

method

1. Bring a stockpot of salted water to a boil. Add the spinach and onion and cook until tender, about 5 minutes. With a slotted spoon, remove spinach and onions. Place in a clean cotton kitchen towel and squeeze to remove excess water.
2. In a medium bowl combine spinach mixture with three Boursin® cheeses. Season to taste. In a small bowl, combine the egg and the water.
3. Lay 12 wonton skins on a lightly floured surface. Keep all but 4 of them covered with a very lightly moistened towel. Brush edges of the 4 exposed wonton skins with egg mixture. Pile a heaping mound of spinach-cheese mixture in the center of each wonton skin, being careful to leave a ½-inch border of dough around filling. Place wonton skins on top to cover the filling on each ravioli. Gently press around filling of each one to conform to its shape, then press firmly to seal edges. Repeat with the remaining wonton skins until you have 12 ravioli.

4. In a large sauté pan, bring cream, pasta sauce, and vodka to a boil. Reduce heat; simmer, stirring occasionally, until thick, about 5 minutes. Season to taste.
5. Add ravioli to the boiling water and stir very gently so they don't stick to the pot or to each other. Cook until pasta is tender and filling warm, about 3 minutes. Carefully drain ravioli in a colander. Add basil and pasta to sauce and gently toss. Drizzle with olive oil and sprinkle with Parmigiano-Reggiano cheese.

the fix
Rob went a little crazy with the salt and pepper (I think he was nervous), so we just diluted the vodka sauce with more of the tomato-basil pasta sauce.

POTATO **GNOCCHI** WITH WILD MUSHROOMS

Donna Stabile was afraid her boyfriend would leave her when she was diagnosed with breast cancer. Instead, he took exquisite care of her—and proposed on her last day of treatment. How do you thank someone for that? He's not a material guy, so she made him a really nice meal. **makes 2 servings**

ingredients

1 4-ounce package dried porcini mushrooms
2 large Idaho potatoes, scrubbed
1 cup pastry flour
   Salt and freshly ground pepper
3 tablespoons Bertolli® extra-virgin olive oil
4 garlic cloves, chopped
8 ounces sliced white button mushrooms
⅓ cup dry red wine
1 cup vegetable stock
8 tablespoons unsalted butter (1 stick)
⅓ cup chopped fresh flat-leaf parsley
1 2-ounce wedge Pecorino Toscano cheese or Parmigiano-Reggiano cheese

method

1. Place porcini mushrooms in a bowl; cover with 2 cups water. Soak overnight. Remove mushrooms. Strain liquid through a coffee filter to remove dirt and sand; reserve each separately.

2. Place a steamer in a large pasta pot. Add enough water so it reaches just under the bottom of the steamer. Cover and bring water to a boil. When steam appears, add potatoes to the pot. Cover; steam potatoes until completely tender, about 1 hour.

3. Peel potatoes and pass through a ricer while piping hot. Spread potatoes on a baking sheet and let cool slightly, about 3 minutes. Sprinkle flour over potatoes. Season with salt and pepper. Using your hands, work flour into potatoes to form a smooth dough. Knead dough about 1 minute, or until it just comes together.

4. On a floured surface, roll handfuls of dough into ¾-inch-thick ropes. Cut into 1-inch-long pieces. Place on a parchment-lined baking sheet; refrigerate until ready to cook.

4. Bring a stockpot of salted water to a boil. Meanwhile, heat olive oil in a large sauté pan over medium heat. Add garlic and cook until fragrant, about 1 minute. Add white mushrooms and cook until golden brown, about 7 minutes. Season with salt and pepper. Add wine and cook, stirring occasionally, until reduced by half, about 7 minutes. Add porcini mushrooms and liquid, along with vegetable stock. Simmer until mushrooms are tender and about one-fourth of the liquid remains. Stir 4 tablespoons of the butter into the sauce. Add parsley and season with salt and pepper.

5. Add gnocchi to the boiling water, stirring so they don't stick. Place remaining 4 tablespoons butter in a large bowl. As gnocchi rise to the top of the pot, remove with a slotted spoon and add to bowl with the butter. Toss cooked gnocchi with butter and parsley; season with salt and pepper.

6. Spoon mushroom sauce over gnocchi. Shave cheese over the top with a vegetable peeler; serve.

the fix

Gnocchi dough is tricky. For starters, I use pastry flour to make the gnocchi more tender. Donna's didn't work out so well. They didn't hold their shape. Instead of shaping by hand, you can put the dough in a pastry bag and pipe it onto the back of a sheet pan in long lines. Freeze for 10 minutes, then cut in small pieces and cook. You can also add a beaten egg for each pound of dough to help them hold together better.

CREAMY PROSCIUTTO **GNOCCHI** WITH TOASTED WALNUTS & PEAS

Putting perfectly cured and aged prosciutto in a cooked dish is not something I always recommend, but it does add an elegant sweet/salty touch to creamy sauces. **makes 4 servings**

grocery list

fresh

8 ounces sliced prosciutto

packaged

Two 17.5-ounce packages Rienzi® fresh potato gnocchi

24-ounce jar Bertolli® Alfredo Sauce with Aged Parmesan Cheese

10-ounce package frozen peas

8-ounce bag walnuts

1 bunch fresh basil

staples

Parmigiano-Reggiano cheese

tools

stockpot

Dutch oven

ingredients

1½ pounds Rienzi® fresh potato gnocchi
    Salt and freshly ground pepper
1   24-ounce jar Bertolli® Alfredo Sauce with Aged Parmesan Cheese
1½ cups frozen peas
8   ounces sliced prosciutto, cut into ½-inch-wide ribbons
1½ cups roughly chopped walnuts, toasted
⅔   cup chopped fresh basil
1   cup grated Parmigiano-Reggiano cheese

method

1. Cook gnocchi in a stockpot of boiling salted water according to package directions. Reserve ½ cup gnocchi-cooking water.
2. Meanwhile, in a Dutch oven heat Alfredo sauce and reserved cooking water over medium heat. When simmering, add peas. Cook until peas are tender, about 2 minutes. Stir in prosciutto, walnuts, and basil.
3. Add gnocchi and toss to coat. Stir in cheese. Season to taste with salt and pepper.

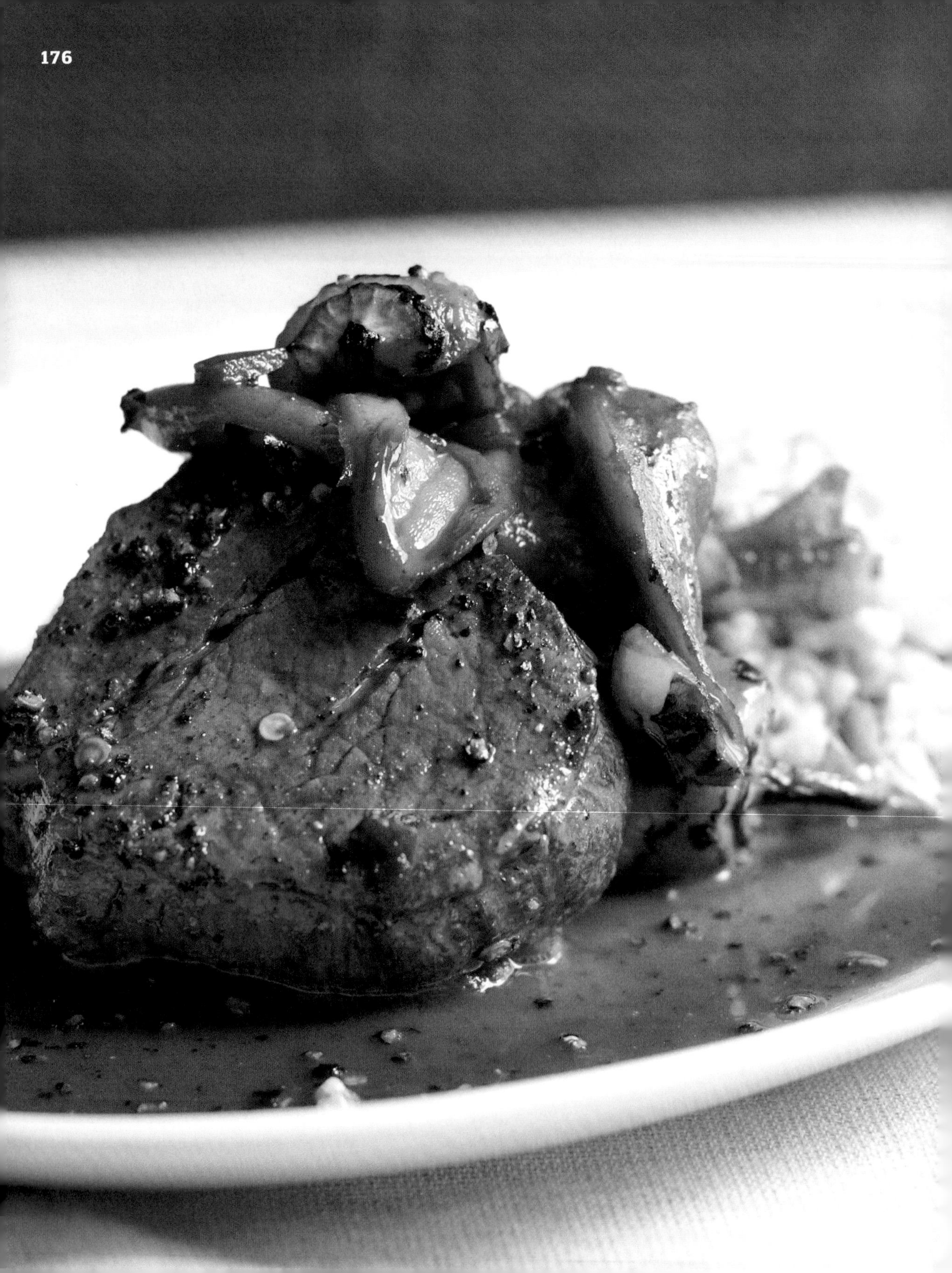

"I started to **EAT HEALTHY** because I wanted to do a triathlon. Whatever your reason, you can do it. Just make one small change at a time.**"**

SPICY **TUNA** WITH COUSCOUS & CARROTS

Any time you take sodium out of a recipe, it's a good idea to add heat for flavor—but a little bit goes a long way. Put in a micro-pinch of cayenne pepper for every teaspoon of sodium you take out.

makes 4 servings

ingredients

2 14-ounce cans low-sodium chicken broth
1½ cups couscous
⅔ cup roughly chopped pitted mixed Mediterranean olives
    Salt and freshly ground pepper
1½ 13.5-ounce pouches Bertolli® Premium Sun-Ripened Tomato & Olive pasta sauce
1 teaspoon crushed red pepper
1½ pounds fresh tuna, cut into bite-size chunks
1 14.5-ounce can baby carrots, drained
½ cup chopped fresh flat-leaf parsley

method

1. In a medium saucepan, bring 2 cups of the chicken broth to a simmer. Stir in the couscous. Cover and remove from heat. Let stand 5 minutes. Fluff with a fork and stir in olives. Season to taste with salt and pepper.

2. Meanwhile, in a large saucepan bring remaining chicken broth, pasta sauce, and crushed red pepper to a gentle boil. Season tuna with salt and pepper; add to the sauce, along with the carrots. Turn heat down, cover, and simmer until tuna is just cooked through, 3 to 4 minutes.

3. Season to taste with salt and pepper, if necessary, and stir in parsley. Serve on a bed of couscous.

grocery list

fresh

1½ pounds fresh tuna

1 bunch flat-leaf parsley

packaged

12-ounce box couscous

12-ounce jar mixed Mediterranean olives

Two 13.5-ounce pouches Bertolli® Premium Sun-Ripened Tomato & Olive pasta sauce

14.5-ounce can baby carrots

staples

low-sodium chicken broth

crushed red pepper

tools

1 medium and
1 large saucepan

POACHED **SALMON** WITH BEETS, LEMON & BROILED STRING BEANS

String beans and salmon are so pretty together. You can't replace the taste of fresh string beans, but beets are another story. This is one of my favorite brands of prepared beets. **makes 4 servings**

grocery list

fresh

1 pound fresh green beans

1¼ pounds skinless salmon fillet

1 bunch chives

packaged

3.15-ounce tube Amore® garlic paste

16-ounce jar Aunt Nellie's® Harvard beets

staples

extra-virgin olive oil

low-sodium chicken broth

lemons

tools

rimmed baking sheet

Dutch oven

ingredients

1   pound fresh green beans, stems removed

2   tablespoons Bertolli® extra-virgin olive oil

1   tablespoon Amore® garlic paste, or 3 garlic cloves, chopped

Salt and freshly ground pepper

1   16-ounce jar Aunt Nellie's® Harvard beets

1   cup low-sodium chicken broth

1¼   pounds skinless salmon fillet, cut into bite-size chunks

Juice and zest of 2 lemons

⅓   cup chopped fresh chives

method

1. Preheat broiler on low. Line a rimmed baking sheet with foil. In a large bowl, toss green beans with oil, garlic paste, and salt and pepper to taste. Spread out on the prepared baking sheet and broil until lightly browned and tender, about 7 minutes.

2. Meanwhile, in a Dutch oven combine beets (and their liquid) and chicken broth; bring to a simmer over high heat. Season salmon generously with salt and pepper. Turn heat down to low and add salmon to the pot. Cover and poach until salmon is barely cooked through, about 4 minutes.

3. Add lemon juice and zest and chives. Season to taste with salt and pepper, if necessary. Divide salmon mixture among four large serving bowls; top with beans.

CHICKEN & FRESH SALSA STEW WITH BLACK BEANS & SOUR CREAM

It's easy to cook without fat in terms of method, but how do you replace the rich flavor? Adding beans—with their buttery, creamy quality—is a good way to do it. **makes 4 servings**

ingredients

3   14-ounce cans low-sodium chicken broth
1   bunch scallions, sliced on a bias (see how-to photos, page 21)
2   15-ounce cans black beans, rinsed and drained
3   boneless, skinless chicken breasts, cut into thin strips
    Salt and freshly ground pepper
2   cups fresh prepared hot salsa
½   cup chopped fresh cilantro
½   cup reduced-fat sour cream

method

1. In a medium saucepan, bring chicken broth, scallions, and black beans to a simmer; turn heat to low.
2. Season chicken with salt and pepper; add to broth. Poach chicken until just cooked through, 2 to 3 minutes. Add salsa and cilantro; season to taste with salt and pepper, if necessary.
3. Ladle stew into bowls, top with a dollop of sour cream, and serve.

grocery list

fresh

1 bunch scallions

3 boneless, skinless chicken breasts

16 ounces prepared hot salsa

1 bunch cilantro

packaged

Two 15-ounce cans black beans

staples

low-sodium chicken broth

reduced-fat sour cream

tools

medium saucepan

CHICKEN & WHITE BEAN SOUP WITH SPINACH & PARMESAN

To make soups and stews low in fat, you can skip the sautéing step where fat is added. Just bring all the ingredients to a simmer together—and serve. **makes 4 servings**

grocery list

fresh

3 boneless, skinless
chicken breasts

packaged

13.5-ounce pouch Bertolli®
Premium Summer
Crushed Tomato & Basil
pasta sauce

15-ounce can cannellini
beans

6-ounce package
prewashed baby spinach

1-ounce package fresh
basil

staples

low-sodium chicken broth

crushed red pepper

Parmigiano-Reggiano
cheese

tools

Dutch oven

ingredients

3 14-ounce cans low-sodium
   chicken broth
1 13.5-ounce pouch Bertolli®
   Premium Summer Crushed
   Tomato & Basil pasta sauce
1 15-ounce can cannellini
   beans (or other white
   beans), rinsed and drained
¾ teaspoon crushed red pepper
3 boneless, skinless chicken
   breasts, sliced thin
   Salt and freshly ground
   pepper
1 6-ounce package prewashed
   baby spinach
½ cup chopped fresh basil
¾ cup grated Parmigiano-
   Reggiano cheese

method

1. In a Dutch oven, bring chicken broth, pasta sauce, beans, and crushed red pepper to a simmer. Turn heat to low.
2. Season chicken with salt and pepper and add to the broth. Gently poach the chicken, stirring occasionally, for about 2 minutes (the broth should barely simmer).
3. Stir in spinach and continue to cook until spinach is wilted and chicken is just cooked through, about 2 more minutes. Stir in basil and season to taste with salt and pepper, if necessary.
4. Ladle soup into 4 large bowls and top with cheese.

CHICKEN ALFREDO

When Kelly said chicken Alfredo was the dish I had to remake, I thought, "No way.'" All-natural, fat-free, sodium-free chicken Alfredo sounded elusive, to say the least. With a little ingenuity, I was able to duplicate the creaminess of the real deal—and even finagle some pasta into it. **makes 4 servings**

ingredients

1	Vidalia onion, cut into small dice
6	garlic cloves, finely chopped
1½	cups low-sodium organic free-range chicken broth
¾	pound quinoa pasta
4	5-ounce chicken breasts, pounded thin
	Freshly ground pepper and Nu-Salt®
2	cups chickpea flour, for dredging
3	egg whites, lightly whisked
	Nonstick cooking spray
4	slices turkey bacon, cut into lardons (see how-to photos, page 73)
2	12-ounce cans evaporated fat-free milk
3	tablespoons cornstarch
2	3.25-ounce packages Birds Eye® Steamfresh™ Sweet Peas
4	tablespoons grated Parmigiano-Reggiano cheese
	Generous pinch nutmeg

method

1. In a medium saucepan, combine onion, garlic, and chicken broth. Cover; simmer until onions are tender and liquid reduces, about 20 minutes. Puree in a blender and strain, if desired; set aside.

2. Cook pasta according to package instructions; drain.

3. Meanwhile, season chicken breasts with pepper and Nu-Salt®. Dredge chicken in chickpea flour, then dip in egg whites to thoroughly coat. Dredge again in chickpea flour.

4. Heat a large nonstick skillet over medium heat and spray with nonstick cooking spray. Add chicken and cook until golden brown and just cooked through, 2 to 3 minutes per side. Remove from pan; cover lightly with foil to keep warm.

5. Add turkey bacon to the pan and cook for 1 to 2 minutes. Add 1½ cans of the evaporated milk and bring to a simmer.

6. Meanwhile, mix remaining half can milk with the cornstarch until smooth. Whisk into the pan and add the reserved onion-garlic puree. Add the peas and bring to a simmer. Cook until peas are tender, about 2 minutes.

7. Stir in the cheese and nutmeg. Season to taste with pepper and Nu-Salt®.

8. To serve, make a bed of pasta and lay chicken on top. Spoon sauce over chicken and pasta.

JERK **PORK** CHOPS WITH YAMS & RICE

Warm, earthy spices like cinnamon, fresh herbs, and marinades bring layers of flavor to a healthy dish like this one. **makes 4 servings**

grocery list

fresh

Four bone-in pork chops (about 1¾ pounds)

packaged

12-ounce bottle Lawry's® Caribbean Jerk Marinade

Two 8.8-ounce packages Uncle Ben's® Original Long-Grain White Ready Rice®

40-ounce can cut yams

1-ounce package fresh thyme leaves

staples

vegetable oil

ground cinnamon

tools

grill pan

large cast-iron skillet

ingredients

4   bone-in pork chops, about 1¾ pounds total
¾   cup Lawry's® Caribbean Jerk Marinade
    Salt and freshly ground pepper
2   8.8-ounce packages Uncle Ben's® Original Long-Grain White Ready Rice®
2   tablespoons vegetable oil
1   40-ounce can cut yams, drained
1   teaspoon ground cinnamon
1   tablespoon fresh chopped thyme leaves

method

1. Place pork chops in a resealable plastic bag. Pour ½ cup of the jerk marinade over the chops. Seal and marinate chops for 30 minutes at room temperature or overnight in the refrigerator. Remove chops from bag and discard marinade.
2. Heat grill/grill pan/broiler on high. Season chops with salt and pepper. Grill until just charred and just cooked through, 4 to 5 minutes per side.
3. Meanwhile, heat rice in pouches according to package directions.
4. In a large cast-iron skillet or large sauté pan, heat vegetable oil over high heat. Add sweet potatoes, cinnamon, and thyme. Season to taste with salt and pepper. Cook, stirring occasionally, until sweet potatoes become golden brown and are hot throughout, about 4 minutes.
5. Stir in the remaining ¼ cup marinade; season to taste with salt and pepper, if necessary.
6. To serve, make a bed of rice on a platter and top with sweet potato mixture. Lay pork chops on top of potatoes and serve.

BEEF TENDERLOIN WITH LOADED BAKED YAMS

On this episode, the request was for prime rib au jus with a baked potato and sour cream. I swapped high-fat ribeye for tenderloin and a baked yam loaded with light sour cream and salsa for the baking potato. Nothing missing but the calories. **makes 4 servings**

ingredients

4   small yams
1   large Vidalia onion, cut
      into ⅓-inch-thick rings
      Nonstick cooking spray
1½ cups low-sodium organic
      free-range chicken broth
4   medium tomatillos, husks
      removed
½   Vidalia onion, chopped fine
⅓   cup fresh chopped cilantro
      Juice of 1 lime
      Freshly ground pepper and
      Nu-Salt®
4   5-ounce portions lean beef
      tenderloin
¾   cup light sour cream
¼   cup chopped fresh chives
1   garlic clove, chopped fine
1   tablespoon chopped fresh
      flat-leaf parsley
4   slices turkey bacon,
      cooked according
      to package directions
      and crumbled

method

1. Preheat oven to 350°F. Bake yams until tender, about 1 hour.
2. Heat grill on high. Spray onion rings with nonstick cooking spray; grill until charred, about 4 minutes per side. In a small saucepan combine grilled onions with chicken broth. Cover and simmer until onions are tender, about 6 minutes.
3. Char tomatillos on the grill until mostly black, turning often. Cool slightly; rub off skin with clean paper towels; roughly chop. Combine with chopped onion, cilantro, and lime juice; season with Nu-Salt®.
4. Meanwhile, heat a medium sauté pan over medium-high heat. Season steaks with pepper and Nu-Salt®; spray pan with nonstick cooking spray. Cook steaks 4 minutes per side for medium rare. Remove from pan; let rest.

5. In a food processor or blender, puree the onion-broth mixture; strain through a fine-mesh strainer into a bowl. Discard solids; season onion jus to taste with pepper and Nu-Salt®.
6. In a bowl combine sour cream, chives, garlic, and parsley. Season to taste. Serve steaks with onion jus and the baked yams topped with herbed sour cream, tomatillo salsa, and bacon.

PEPPER **STEAK**

The probability that I could make a low-fat/low-sodium/sugar-free version of a popular dish like pepper steak and like it BETTER than the original is less than low, but that's exactly what happened here. This is sooo good! **makes 4 servings**

ingredients

3½ cups low-sodium, organic free-range chicken broth
Nu-Salt® and freshly ground pepper
1 cup short-grain brown rice
1 tablespoon Bertolli® extra-virgin olive oil
12 Anaheim peppers
4 5-ounce portions lean beef tenderloin
Nonstick cooking spray
1 Vidalia onion, thinly sliced
5 cloves garlic, chopped
3 tablespoons balsamic vinegar
3 tablespoons cornstarch
½ cup Trader Joe's® Organic Marinara Sauce (No Salt, Fat Free)
½ cup evaporated fat-free milk
Pinch cayenne
½ cup chopped fines herbes (a mix of parsley, chives, tarragon, and chervil)

method

1. In a medium saucepan, bring 2 cups of the chicken broth to a boil over high heat. Season with Nu-Salt®; add rice. Cover and turn heat down to low. Cook until rice is tender and liquid is absorbed, about 1 hour. Fluff rice with a fork. Toss with oil; cover.

2. In a well-ventilated area, heat a grill pan over medium-high heat. When pan is hot, place peppers on it (if your grill pan isn't large enough to accommodate all of the peppers, do this in stages). Grill peppers, turning occasionally, until pepper skins are charred, about 12 to 15 minutes. Place peppers in a bowl and cover with plastic wrap for about 7 minutes to steam off skin.

3. Trim the tops and bottoms off peppers. (See how-to photos, page 191.) Cut a slit down one side of each pepper; open it up. Scrape out the seeds and membranes with a knife. Turn the pepper over and scrape off as much of the charred skin as possible. Cut the flattened peppers, from top to bottom, into wide strips. Cut each strip into ½-inch-thick strips.

5. Heat a large sauté pan over medium-high heat. Season steaks with Nu-Salt® and pepper. Spray pan with cooking spray. Cook steaks until golden brown, about 4 minutes per side. Remove from pan; cover lightly with foil.

6. Spray pan again with cooking spray; add onions. Cook and stir until onions are just tender, about 5 minutes. Add garlic; cook and stir for 1 minute. Add vinegar; scrape bits that are stuck in pan.

7. Add 1 cup of the chicken broth; bring to a simmer. Mix the remaining ½ cup chicken broth with cornstarch. Whisk into the pan. Stir in the marinara and evaporated milk; bring to a simmer. Add peppers and cayenne; simmer until vegetables are tender, 3 to 4 minutes.

8. Return beef to the pan to reheat, about 2 minutes. Stir in herbs. Serve with rice.

1. Start by removing the tops and bottoms of the charred peppers with a sharp knife.

2. Cut a slit in each pepper, then lay the peppers flat. Scrape the seeds and membranes from the insides. Turn the peppers over, so the charred outside is facing up.

3. Carefully scrape off as much of the charred black skin as possible; discard the charred skin. Resist the urge to rinse the peppers because good flavor will wash away.

4. Using a sharp knife, cut the peppers lengthwise into wide strips. Pile the strips on top of one another, then cut those strips into smaller ½-inch strips. Set strips aside.

MINT CHOCOLATE CHIP FROZEN **YOGURT**

Ice cream addict and *Biggest Loser* contestant Mark went gaga over this nonfat ice-cream replacement. Gelatin and skim milk replicate the creamy texture of high-fat ice cream, while cocoa nibs add crunch and intense chocolate flavor without the sugar. **makes 4 servings**

ingredients

- 2 teaspoons powdered gelatin
- 1¾ cups skim milk
- 1 cup Splenda®
- 1 17.6-ounce container
  Total 10% Fage® yogurt
- ½ teaspoon organic
  peppermint extract
  Green food coloring
- ¼ cup cocoa nibs or one,
  1-ounce 99%-cocoa
  chocolate bar, finely
  chopped

method

1. In a large mixing bowl, sprinkle gelatin over ½ cup of the milk.
2. In a small saucepan, heat the remaining 1¼ cups milk with Splenda over medium-high heat, stirring frequently. When mixture is boiling, pour into the bowl with milk and gelatin and stir until gelatin is dissolved.
3. Stir yogurt into gelatin mixture. Whisk in peppermint extract and enough green food coloring to reach desired color.
4. Freeze in an ice cream machine according to manufacturer's instructions. Toward the end of freezing time, add chocolate. Serve immediately or freeze to desired consistency.

"

The **HOLIDAYS** are as much about food as anything else. It's the time to discover your inner chef and indulge—in cooking and eating. **"**

24-HOUR **TURKEY**

A fresh-herb marinade serves double duty here. It flavors the bird overnight, then cooks with it in the oven to create almost instant, preseasoned gravy. **makes 20 servings**

ingredients

8 cups low-sodium chicken broth
2 cups dry white wine
1 tablespoon salt, plus more for seasoning
1 teaspoon black peppercorns
3 tablespoons sugar
2 onions, cut into medium chunks
15 garlic cloves, peeled
1 parsnip, peeled and cut into medium chunks
3 carrots, peeled and cut into medium chunks
2 white turnips, peeled and cut into medium chunks
1 bunch fresh flat-leaf parsley, leaves roughly chopped
1 bunch fresh sage, leaves roughly chopped
1 bunch fresh rosemary, leaves roughly chopped
1 bunch fresh thyme, leaves roughly chopped
2 to 3 bay leaves
⅔ cup Bertolli® extra-virgin olive oil, plus more for brushing
1 13-pound turkey (thawed, if frozen), giblet bag and neck removed and reserved
  Freshly ground pepper
6 tablespoons cornstarch

method

1. In an extra-large mixing bowl (about 8 quarts), combine broth, wine, the 1 tablespoon salt, peppercorns, sugar, onions, garlic, parsnip, carrots, turnips, fresh herbs, and bay leaves.
2. Put turkey in a clean, unscented garbage bag; pour marinade over. Twist bag and seal with an extra-large twist tie or tie with twine. Place in a very large bowl and refrigerate for about 18 hours.
3. Preheat oven to 200°F. Remove turkey from marinade. Remove vegetables from marinade, reserving each separately. In a large saucepan combine marinade, giblets, and neck. Simmer, uncovered, for 1 hour. Strain, reserving broth. (You should have 4 to 5 cups of broth.)
4. Toss vegetables with the ⅔ cup olive oil and spread in the bottom of a large, heavy, flameproof roasting pan. Place turkey on a roasting rack on top of vegetables. Season turkey with salt and freshly ground pepper. Roast for 3½ hours, rotating pan every hour. Turn oven to 425°F. Brush turkey with olive oil; roast for another 45 to 55 minutes, or until skin is golden brown and meat is just cooked through.
5. Remove turkey from the pan and place on a carving board or serving platter. Cover lightly with foil and let rest for 30 minutes

while you make the gravy. (If vegetables aren't tender, return them to the oven and continue to roast until they are done.)
6. Remove vegetables from roasting pan; cover lightly with foil to keep warm. Pour all but 1 cup of the strained broth into the roasting pan and bring to a simmer over medium heat. In a medium bowl, whisk remaining broth with cornstarch. Slowly whisk cornstarch mixture into boiling broth. Cook, whisking, over medium heat until gravy consistency is achieved, about 2 minutes. Strain and season to taste. Return vegetables to gravy.
7. Carve turkey and serve with vegetable gravy.

Quick Cranberry Relish

1 pound fresh cranberries
⅔ cup granulated sugar
  Zest of 2 limes
  Zest of 2 oranges
  Pinch of salt

1. In the bowl of a food processor, combine cranberries, sugar, lime zest, orange zest, and salt; process to chop fine.
2. Transfer to a serving bowl and cover with plastic wrap. Refrigerate for 2 hours to allow sugar to dissolve and flavors to develop. (If you'd like to serve this relish immediately, you can heat it in a medium saucepan until all of the sugar is dissolved.)

THE GREAT **TURKEY** LEFTOVER SOUP

Everyone has their version of a post-Thanksgiving pot of soup. This one makes use of leftover stuffing, too: Mix it with a little beaten egg, and make dumplings with it. **makes 4 servings**

ingredients

2 cups leftover stuffing
3 whole eggs, beaten
2 tablespoons unsalted butter
1 cup small dice of pumpkin or butternut squash
½ large Vidalia onion, diced
2 tablespoons Amore® garlic paste, or 4 cloves garlic, chopped
   Salt and freshly ground pepper
1 32-ounce container organic chicken broth
2 tablespoons chopped fresh sage
1 pound shredded leftover turkey meat
3 tablespoons freshly grated Parmigiano-Reggiano cheese

method

1. In a medium bowl, combine leftover stuffing with eggs. Let sit for a few minutes to allow stuffing to absorb the eggs.

2. Meanwhile, in a Dutch oven heat butter over medium-high heat. Add pumpkin and onion to the pan. Cook for about 5 minutes, stirring often, until vegetables begin to soften. Stir garlic paste into the vegetables; season to taste with salt and pepper. Continue to cook until vegetables are tender, about 5 more minutes. Add chicken broth and sage to the pot and bring to a simmer.

3. Using about 2 tablespoons of the stuffing mixture, form a dumpling. Repeat with remaining stuffing mixture. Gently drop dumplings into simmering broth and allow to cook until set, about 3 minutes.

4. Add turkey to the soup. Season to taste with salt and pepper, if necessary. When soup is hot throughout, ladle into bowls. Top with cheese and serve.

> **❝THANKSGIVING** is so great. It's about gratitude not attitude. It's about cooking, eating, and gathering with the friends and family I love. **❞**

APPLE PIE WITH CINNAMON & ROSEMARY

The fresh rosemary is an Italian touch in an all-American classic. The Italians flavor rustic cakes—
sometimes made with polenta—with rosemary. It adds a little astringency, and an almost citrusy flavor
and aroma to this pie. **makes 8 servings**

ingredients

For the crust
2½ cups all-purpose flour, plus
    more for rolling crust
1 teaspoon salt
1 tablespoon sugar
1 cup unsalted butter, cut into
    chunks and frozen
⅓ cup ice water

For the filling
10 Granny Smith apples
½ cup sugar
3 tablespoons cornstarch
2 tablespoons ground
    cinnamon
2 tablespoons chopped fresh
    rosemary
1 teaspoon salt
1 egg, beaten
    Turbinado sugar

method

1. Preheat oven to 400°F.
2. For the crust: Place the flour, salt, and sugar in bowl of food processor and pulse to combine. Pulse in butter until it resembles coarse meal. With machine on, drizzle in water, a little at a time, until dough just holds together without being wet or sticky. Divide dough in half and shape into 2 flat disks. Wrap tightly in plastic wrap and refrigerate for at least ½ hour.
3. On a lightly floured surface roll out one disk into a 12-inch circle about ⅛ inch thick. Carefully transfer to a 9-inch pie dish.
4. Peel and core apples and cut each one into 8 to 10 wedges. Toss apples with sugar, cornstarch, cinnamon, rosemary, and salt.

Pile into lined pie dish. Roll out remaining dough on a lightly floured surface into a 12-inch circle about ⅛ inch thick. Gently place on top of apples; press gently to conform to the shape of the apples. With a pair of kitchen shears, trim excess dough to about ½ inch around entire pie. Press gently to seal; crimp if desired. (To crimp the edge, place one thumb against the inside edge of the pastry. With the thumb and index finger of your other hand, press the pastry from the outside edge into your first thumb to create a crimp. Repeat around perimeter of pie. Alternatively, cut free form leaf shapes from the rolled-out top crust, scoring them with the tip of a paring knife. Arrange decoratively over the top of the pie.)
5. Brush beaten egg over entire surface of the pie. Sprinkle generously with turbinado sugar. Bake until golden brown and apples are tender, about 1¼ hours. Cool on a wire rack. (If you want to serve it warm, let it cool for 1½ to 2 hours, then serve.)

"

CHRISTMAS EVE
is the highlight
of the year for
my family. It
attracts the biggest
crowd, gets the
most money spent
on it, and has
the best meal. "

FRITTURA

"Frittura" may simply mean "fried food" in Italian, but at my mom's house, it refers to a big pile of crisp, sweet little fish and rings of calamari. Good with a squeeze of lemon too. **makes 4 servings**

ingredients

3 quarts vegetable oil
2 cups Bertolli® Summer Crushed Tomato and Basil pasta sauce
1 teaspoon crushed red pepper
½ pound whitebait or smelts
3 cups chickpea flour, for dredging
Salt and freshly ground pepper
½ pound calamari, cleaned and cut into ⅓-inch rings

method

1. In a large pasta pot heat oil over high heat to 375°F to 400°F.
2. In a medium saucepan, combine pasta sauce and crushed red pepper. Heat until warm.
3. Meanwhile, dredge fish in chickpea flour. Shake off excess flour and add to the oil. Fry until pale golden brown, stirring often, about 2 minutes. Remove from oil with a slotted skimmer and drain on paper towels. Season generously with salt and pepper.
4. Repeat process with calamari, (dredging in chickpea flour first) but fry for about 3 minutes.
5. Serve fried fish with warm sauce.

▶ My brother, Michael (right), and I sit for our annual Christmas portrait with the May's Department Store Santa in Jamaica, Queens, in 1971.

ZUPPA DI **PESCE**

There are many variations of this Italian fish soup—certainly the types of fish used depend on what's freshest and most available—but almost every version contains both fish and shellfish, tomatoes in some form, and white wine. **makes 4 servings**

ingredients

3   tablespoons Bertolli® extra-virgin olive oil
1   large head fennel, trimmed, cored and sliced thin
    Salt and freshly ground pepper
⅔   teaspoon saffron threads
1   cup dry white wine
1   16-ounce container Pacific® Red Pepper and Tomato Soup
2   cups roughly chopped canned plum tomatoes
¾   pound snapper fillet, cut into 1-inch chunks
½   pound raw shrimp, peeled and deveined (see how-to photos, page 145)
½   cup chopped fresh flat-leaf parsley

method

1. In a Dutch oven, heat olive oil over medium heat. Add fennel; season with salt and pepper. Cook, stirring occasionally, until tender, about 6 minutes. Add saffron and white wine and bring to a simmer. Cook until wine is reduced by half, about 3 minutes.

2. Add soup and tomatoes to pan and bring to a simmer. Turn heat to low and cover. Season snapper and shrimp with salt and pepper and stir into soup. Cover and gently poach fish until just cooked through, about 4 minutes.

3. Stir in parlsey. Season to taste with salt and pepper, if necessary.

PERSIMMON POUND **CAKE**

Few things are as dramatic as a flaming dessert, tableside. (The term for it is "flambé.") Just exercise care and watch your hair—and you'll get LOTS of applause. **makes 12 servings**

ingredients

1½ cups plus 2 tablespoons unsalted butter, at room temperature

2 cups plus ¾ cup granulated sugar

6 eggs

½ cup persimmon puree (3 to 4 peeled persimmons, pureed in a blender)

3½ cups cake flour, sifted

½ teaspoon baking powder

1 teaspoon salt

2 tablespoons sour cream
Pinch nutmeg

3 cups chestnuts in syrup, drained, or 3 cups roasted and peeled chestnuts (half of them roughly chopped)

¾ cup water

¾ cup brandy

method

1. Preheat oven to 350°F.
2. In the bowl of a stand mixer fitted with the paddle attachment, beat butter and the 2 cups sugar on medium-high speed until light and fluffy, about 3 minutes. With machine running, add eggs one at a time, beating well after each addition. Scrape bowl with a rubber or silicone spatula. Add persimmon puree; beat until thoroughly blended. With mixer on low, add flour, baking powder, and salt until just blended. Scrape bowl again and mix in sour cream, nutmeg, and the 1½ chopped chestnuts.
3. Grease the bottom and sides of a bundt pan. Pour batter in the pan and bake until a cake tester or toothpick inserted in the center of the cake comes out clean, 45 to 50 minutes.
4. While the cake is baking, make the glaze: Cut the remaining chestnuts in half. In a medium saucepan, combine the ¾ cup sugar and the water. Bring to a boil over medium heat. Cook, stirring

frequently, until mixture develops a syrupy consistency, about 5 minutes. Remove it from the heat and add the halved chestnuts. Set aside in a warm place until the cake is done baking.
5. When the cake is done, remove it from oven and let cool on a wire rack for 10 minutes. Invert onto a serving plate. Ladle the chestnut syrup over the top of the cake, letting the nuts scatter. (If the glaze is not of a pouring consistency, warm it with 2 tablespoons of water until it loosens up.)
6. At the table, douse the top of the cake with the brandy. Immediately (and very carefully), light the alcohol with a lit match or candle lighter. When the flames go out, cut into slices and serve.

STRUFOLI

These brightly decorated, fried honey balls are classic Southern Italy. They're part sweets, part arts and crafts—and very festive by design. **makes 12 servings**

ingredients

9   eggs
¾   cup Bertolli® extra-virgin
      olive oil
5½ cups all-purpose flour, plus
      more for kneading
      Vegetable oil, for frying
¼   cup honey
1   to 1½ cups granulated sugar
      Confetti sprinkles
      Sliced almonds

method

1. In a large bowl, beat eggs and oil thoroughly with a whisk.
2. Stir the 5½ cups flour into egg mixture with a wooden spoon. On a lightly floured surface, knead dough for 20 minutes or longer, until soft.
3. Break off a quarter-size piece of dough; cover remaining dough with plastic wrap or a damp kitchen towel to keep from drying out. Roll into a long narrow strip. Cut into scant ½-inch-long pieces.
4. Fill a large, heavy skillet halfway up the sides with vegetable oil. Heat over high heat. When oil is hot, carefully add dough pieces to pan. (Don't overcrowd the pan—put in only a handful at a time. If oil starts to foam, it's too cool; turn up the heat.) Cook

dough until lightly golden brown, about 3 minutes. Drain on a paper towel-lined plate. Repeat with remaining dough.
5. In a large skillet, combine honey and 1 to 1½ cups sugar. Cook, stirring frequently, over high heat until mixture boils. Add cooked pieces of dough, stirring to coat every piece in honey-sugar glaze.
6. Turn glazed dough pieces out onto a work surface and immediately mold into desired shape (traditionally, that's a wreath). Keep a dish of cool water close by for dipping your fingers when they get too warm.
7. Decorate with confetti sprinkles and almond slices.

◀ The "famiglia" celebrates the holidays 1960s style—with great food, wine, and fabulous hairstyles. That's my mother, Nicolina, in the pink blouse, with my Aunt Maria. The tuxedoed Elvis chatting with my Uncle Joe and Aunt Elena behind her is my dad, Raffaele.

> **"** When you're an Italian-American kid, you grab onto the traditions of other cultures you experience in this country. For me **NEW YEAR'S** was one of those. **"**

LILLET SUGAR CUBE **COCKTAIL**

Lillet is a French apéritif wine from Bordeaux that comes in both white and red varieties. This cocktail calls for "blanc," or the white one. I invented this particular drink for CBS' *The Early Show*. If you have any leftover Champagne from midnight merriment, use it. **makes 1 serving**

ingredients

3 sugar cubes
   Dash Angostura bitters
1 2×¾-inch strip orange peel
1 ounce Lillet Blanc
4½ to 5 ounces chilled
   Champagne

method

1. Drop sugar cubes into a champagne flute; add bitters. Squeeze the orange peel into the glass, then run it over the rim of the glass. Drop peel in glass. Add Lillet, then slowly fill with Champagne.

STUFFED **ARTICHOKES**

Artichokes were always reserved for special occasions in my family. They are one of my mother's specialties. Pull off the leaves and scrape the meaty part of each leaf with your two front teeth. When you get through all the leaves, the heart is, many people believe, the best part. **makes 4 servings**

ingredients

½ cup breadcrumbs
½ cup freshly grated
   Parmigiano-Reggiano
   cheese
5 cloves garlic (2 cloves
   chopped, 3 cloves smashed)
3 tablespoons chopped flat-leaf
   parsley
1 teaspoon chopped fresh
   oregano
2 tablespoons plus ¼ cup
   Bertolli® extra-virgin
   olive oil
   Juice and zest of 2 lemons
   Salt and freshly ground
   pepper
4 fresh artichokes
1 sprig fresh thyme
1½ cups dry white wine
1 cup vegetable broth

method

1. For the filling: In a medium bowl, combine breadcrumbs, cheese, chopped garlic, parsley, oregano, the 2 tablespoons olive oil, and lemon zest. Season to taste with salt and pepper.
2. Cut the stems off of the artichokes and pull off the tough outer leaves. Cut about ½ inch off of the top of each artichoke to create a flat top. Make sure the bottoms are flat so the artichokes can stand up. With your fingers, spread the leaves apart as much as you can, stuffing the breadcrumb mixture between them. Put plenty of the filling on top of the artichokes.

3. In a Dutch oven, heat the remaining ¼ cup olive oil over medium heat. Add the smashed garlic cloves to the oil and cook until fragrant, about 1 minute. Add thyme, wine, lemon juice, and vegetable broth. Arrange artichokes in pot, cover, and place over medium heat. Simmer until artichokes are tender throughout, about 30 minutes.

YORKSHIRE **PUDDING**

Traditional Yorkshire pudding is cooked in the beef fat that drips off a roast. These are cooked, popover style, in a popover or muffin pan. **makes 24 servings**

ingredients

4   cups all-purpose flour
1   tablespoon plus 2 teaspoons salt
4   cups milk
8   large eggs
     Nonstick cooking spray
2⅓ cups shredded cheddar cheese, about 10 ounces

method

1. Place a ½-cup popover pan or standard-size muffin tin in the oven. Preheat oven to 350°F.

2. Place the flour and salt in a fine-mesh sieve and sift it onto a piece of wax paper.

3. In a small saucepan, heat the milk over medium heat until small bubbles appear around the edges.

4. In a large bowl, whisk the eggs until frothy. Slowly whisk hot milk into the eggs, being careful not to cook the eggs; set aside.

5. Gradually whisk the dry ingredients into the egg mixture, stirring until almost smooth (a few lumps are fine).

6. Remove the hot popover pan from the oven; spray the cups with nonstick cooking spray. While the pan is still slightly warm or at room temperature, fill each cup at least ¾ full.* Top each pudding with some of the grated cheese. Place pan on a baking sheet to catch any drips.

7. Bake puddings for 15 minutes. Rotate the pan 180° so that the puddings will rise evenly. Bake until puddings are golden brown, about another 35 minutes.

8. Invert the pan to remove the puddings and serve immediately. (Puddings can also be made up to 2 hours in advance. Prick them a few times with a fork to keep them from deflating, then cool on a wire rack. Reheat in a 250° oven for 5 to 6 minutes just before serving.)

*Note: Depending on how many pans you have, you'll have to repeat the filling/baking process the number of times it takes to use all of the batter.

GARLIC & HORSERADISH-CRUSTED STANDING **RIB ROAST** WITH ROOT VEGETABLE & RED WINE GRAVY

Although you don't have to use prime-grade, dry-aged beef, the difference in flavor and texture between it and a standard rib roast is remarkable. **makes 12 servings**

ingredients

for the meat

1   10- to 12-pound prime, dry-aged, bone-in standing rib roast (4 to 5 ribs)

4   tablespoons sea salt
     Freshly ground black pepper

for the crust

10   cloves garlic, peeled and cut into chunks

1   large onion, chopped (about 1 cup)

3   tablespoons prepared horseradish, drained, plus additional for serving

4   tablespoons fresh oregano leaves

3   tablespoons all-purpose flour

½   cup mayonnaise

for roasting

2   medium onions, peeled and cut into large chunks (about 2 cups)

2   carrots, peeled and cut into large chunks (about 1 cup)

1   medium turnip, peeled and cut into large chunks (about 1 cup)

1   small celery root, peeled and cut into large chunks (about 1 cup)

1   head garlic, split into cloves and peeled

2   cups chicken broth

for the gravy

3   strips bacon, cut crosswise into ¼-inch strips (about ½ cup)

3   tablespoons all-purpose flour

1   cup dry red wine

3   cups chicken broth

2   sprigs fresh oregano

method

1. Preheat the oven to 450°F. Season the roast with the sea salt and generous amounts of freshly ground black pepper.

2. For the crust: Place the garlic, onion, 3 tablespoons horseradish, oregano, flour, and mayonnaise in the bowl of a food processor. Pulse until a rough paste forms. Smooth the garlic mixture on the top and sides of the roast.

2. Place the onions, carrots, turnip, celery root, and garlic in a large roasting pan. Pour the chicken broth over the vegetables. Place the roast, crusted side up and rib side down, on top of the vegetables.

3. Insert an oven-safe meat thermometer in the thickest part of the roast (the center of the eye), being careful not to touch the bone. Place roast in the oven and cook at 450° for 15 minutes. Reduce oven temperature to 250° and continue to cook for about 20 minutes per pound.

4. Remove the roast from the oven when the internal temperature reaches 120° for rare, 130° for medium rare, or 140° for medium (or as desired), using the chart on page 211 as a guide.

5. Move the roast to a cutting board and cover it loosely with aluminum foil. Let it stand for a minimum of 30 minutes before

method *(cont.)*

carving. The internal temperature of the roast will continue to rise by about 5°, even after you take it out of the oven.

6. While the roast rests, make the gravy. Pour all of the juices from the pan into a gravy separator to separate the fat from the meat juices. (There is no better way to do this.)

7. Place the roasting pan, with the vegetables in it, on the stovetop over medium-low heat. Add the bacon. When the bacon is warm, add the flour and stir until everything is blended. Continue to cook and stir for 5 minutes. Add the wine to the pan, stirring and scraping up any browned bits. Cook and stir until the wine reduces by half. Add the chicken broth, meat juices, and oregano. Turn the heat down, if necessary, and let gravy simmer on the stovetop for 30 minutes, skimming the fat off the top periodically. You can strain it before serving if you like, but I like the chunky version.

8. While gravy is simmering, remove the fat layer from the roast and trim off the rib bones, if you like. (You may also trim off the tail portion of the roast, depending on its fat content and your cholesterol level.)

9. Using an electric knife, carve the roast at the table. Keep in mind: The outside portions are more done than the inside portions. If you have a portion that's more rare than your guest likes, return it to the pan with the gravy. Cook it on top of the stove for 30 seconds per side—that should do it.

10. Serve the roast with hot gravy (strained or chunky) and prepared horseradish on the side.

Recipe Notes
A few things to ask of your butcher:
First, request the small end of the roast. The larger end comes from the shoulder of the animal and is naturally tougher. Also, ask the butcher to trim the backbone (the chine) off the roast but leave the rib bones connected. Also ask him to trim the fat cap off the roast, but to place it back on top before tying the roast.

A few things you need to know:
● Be sure your roast is at room temperature before placing it in the oven—it won't cook properly in the time and at the temperature allotted if it starts out icebox-cold. Let it sit out, covered with plastic wrap, for 1 hour before cooking.
● Ideally, use a large stainless steel or cast-iron, heavy-bottomed roasting pan to cook the roast. Either is perfect for long, slow, low-temp roasting—and you can put either one on the stovetop to make the gravy.
● No time/temp formula can ever be 100 percent accurate, due to the variables in oven temperatures from kitchen to kitchen. Using an oven-safe meat thermometer is the only way to make sure the roast is cooked to your liking. (See the chart below.)
● All roasts must rest after they are removed from the oven for these temperatures to be accurate and to allow the juices to be reabsorbed into the meat so they don't spill all over the cutting board. A roast this size continues to cook even after it's removed from the oven. It needs 30 to 45 minutes tented with foil in a warm area before carving.
● You will need a gravy separator (the type with the spout attached at the bottom) to make the gravy.

Doneness Chart

Rare	120°F to 125°F
Medium-rare	130°F to 135°F
Medium	140°F to 145°F
Medium-well	150°F to 155°F
Well done	160°F and above

"

The most romantic thing you can do on **VALENTINE'S DAY** is cook for someone. Take the course of the evening into your own hands.

"

LOBSTER WITH LEMONY RED PEPPER BUTTER

Believe it or not, whole boiled lobster is one of the easiest things you can make—and it's sexy and red.
Here, it's served with a hot, sweet, and sour drawn butter. **makes 4 servings**

ingredients

4   1½-pound lobsters
1   9-ounce jar Tracklements
      Chilli Jam
      Juice and zest of 2 lemons
8   tablespoons unsalted butter
      (1 stick)
      Salt and freshly ground
      pepper

method

1. In a pot large enough to hold the 4 lobsters, bring 2 cups of water to a boil. Add lobsters to the pan and cover with a lid. Steam lobsters 8 to 10 minutes or until just cooked through.

2. Meanwhile, in a medium saucepan heat jam, lemon juice, and zest over medium heat until simmering. Whisk in butter and bring back to a simmer. Shut off heat and season with salt and pepper to taste.

3. Serve whole lobsters with cracking utensils and sauce on the side for dipping.

ROASTED SWEET **POTATOES**

The lobster is so rich and kind of extravagant, it doesn't need much accompaniment. You want to keep things really, really simple. These sweet potatoes are very low maintenance—and creamy and yummy. **makes 4 servings**

ingredients

4   large sweet potatoes, scrubbed
8   tablespoons butter
    Salt and freshly ground pepper

method

1. Preheat oven to 350°F. Prick sweet potatoes with fork and wrap tightly with foil.
2. Roast potatoes until tender when tested with a fork, about 1¼ hours.
3. Make a slit in each sweet potato running the length of the potato but not cutting all the way through. Scoop out the flesh of each potato and place in medium bowl; reserve skins.
4. Roughly mash the flesh with the butter until fluffy. Season to taste with salt and pepper. Return flesh to the scooped-out sweet potatoes; rewrap in foil, if desired, and serve warm.

S'MORES **TARTLETS**

How often do you get an excuse to use Fluff? Can't resist it. **makes 4 servings**

ingredients

8 Keebler® Mini Graham
   Cracker Pie Crusts, or
   other tart shells of choice
8 ounces bittersweet
   chocolate, chopped
8 large strawberries, sliced
1½ cups Marshmallow Fluff®
   marshmallow creme
   Salt

method

1. Preheat oven to 400°F.
2. Place tart shells on a baking sheet. Bake until golden brown, about 1½ minutes. Remove from oven and turn oven up to 500°.
3. Meanwhile, in a microwaveable bowl melt chocolate in microwave at 50 percent power for about 3 minutes, or until melted, stirring halfway through cooking time. Spoon a little more than a tablespoon of melted chocolate into the bottom of each tart shell. Arrange strawberry slices from one strawberry on the chocolate in each shell. Spoon about 3 tablespoons Fluff inside each shell and spread to cover the entire surface of the shell. Sprinkle a tiny amount of salt on top of the Fluff.
4. Place filled tartlets in oven. Watching carefully, allow the Fluff to get toasty brown, about 3 minutes. Remove from oven. Place 2 tartlets on each plate. Drizzle with remaining melted chocolate and serve immediately.

ITALIAN EASTER **BREAD**

When it's shaped and baked, this bread looks like a nest full of brightly colored eggs. The eggs cook in the oven, so it makes a great Easter Sunday breakfast: hard-cooked egg and a slice of sweet bread.

makes 1 ring-shaped loaf

ingredients

3 cups all-purpose flour, plus more for kneading dough
2 tablespoons sugar
1 package active dry yeast (2 ¼ teaspoons)
¼ teaspoon salt
⅔ cup warm milk
2 tablespoons butter, softened
7 eggs
Nontoxic egg dye
Vegetable oil

method

1. In a large mixing bowl, whisk together 1 cup of the flour, the sugar, yeast, and salt. Add the milk and butter and beat with an electric mixer on medium speed for 2 minutes. Add 2 of the eggs and another ½ cup flour and beat on high for 2 minutes.

2. Stir in enough remaining flour (about 1½ cups) to form a soft dough. Turn out onto a lightly floured surface and knead until smooth and elastic, 6 to 8 minutes. Place in a greased bowl, turning once to grease the top. Cover with a clean damp kitchen towel or plastic wrap and let rise in a warm place until doubled in size, about 1 hour.

3. While dough is rising, color the remaining 5 (raw) eggs with nontoxic dyes. When they're dry, rub them lightly with vegetable oil.

4. Punch dough down and divide in half. Roll each half into a 24-inch rope. On a lightly oiled baking sheet, loosely braid the ropes together. Form the braid into a ring, pinching the ends together to seal. Gently split the ropes and tuck in the 5 colored eggs, spacing them evenly around the ring. Cover lightly with a clean damp kitchen towel and let rise again until doubled, about 30 minutes.

5. Meanwhile, preheat the oven to 350°F.

6. Bake until golden brown, about 30 to 35 minutes. Remove from baking sheet and cool on a wire rack.

> " For people from the Mediterranean— my clan included— **EASTER** is hugely important. It always involves church, and it always involves lamb. "

ROASTED EASTER **LAMB**

A boneless leg of lamb may be a little simpler to carve, but I prefer bone-in. It's juicier, more flavorful—and makes a gorgeous presentation. **makes 8 servings**

ingredients

- ½ cup white wine vinegar
- ½ teaspoon dried oregano, crushed
- ¾ cup Bertolli® extra-virgin olive oil
- 1 tablespoon salt, plus more for seasoning
- 1½ teaspoons freshly ground pepper, plus more for seasoning
- 1 7- to 9-pound bone-in leg of lamb
- ¼ cup dried breadcrumbs
- 15 small russet potatoes, quartered
- 10 small yellow onions, quartered
- 1 cup chopped fresh flat-leaf parsley, for garnish

method

1. In a medium bowl, combine the vinegar, oregano, ½ cup of the olive oil, the 1 tablespoon salt, and the 1½ teaspoons pepper. Place lamb in a clean 2-gallon resealable plastic bag. Pour marinade over lamb. Seal and place in a large dish. Refrigerate, covered, for 24 hours.

2. Preheat the oven to 350°F. In a large bowl combine the remaining ¼ cup olive oil, breadcrumbs, and salt and pepper to taste. Add potatoes and onions to bowl and toss to thoroughly coat.

3. Remove lamb from the marinade and put in a roasting pan (not on a rack). Discard marinade. Arrange potatoes and onions around lamb.

4. Roast lamb and vegetables, uncovered, until an instant-read thermometer reads 140°F for medium, about 1½ to 2 hours.

5. Cover lightly with foil and let rest for 20 minutes before carving.

6. Sprinkle lamb and vegetables with chopped parsley. Serve lamb with roasted vegetables.

SPRING GREEN SALAD

Tarragon is one of those herbs that takes a little getting used to—it's pretty licorice-y and strong. But I love it. Tastes like spring to me. **makes 4 servings**

ingredients

1½ cups Diner's Choice® mashed sweet potatoes
4 hardboiled eggs
Salt and freshly ground pepper
1 large bunch asparagus, woody ends trimmed
1½ bunches scallions, roots trimmed and sliced in half lengthwise
6 tablespoons butter
Juice and zest of 1½ lemons
3 tablespoons chopped fresh tarragon

method

1. Preheat a grill/grill pan/broiler on high. Bring a large pot of salted water to a boil. Meanwhile, in a microwaveable dish, heat sweet potatoes, covered, in the microwave on high until hot, about 4 minutes. Separate the egg whites from the yolks and chop each finely; set aside separately.

2. To blanch the asparagus: Drop the asparagus into the boiling water and let cook until tender, about 5 minutes. Remove asparagus from pot and drop immediately into a bowl of ice-cold water to stop the cooking process. Drain and set aside.

3. Season scallions with salt and pepper to taste and grill until tender and a little bit charred, turning once. Remove from grill and cut into 2-inch-long pieces.

4. To make lemon-butter sauce: Heat a medium saucepan over medium-high heat; add butter. Cook until butter is a deep golden-brown color; add lemon juice and zest. Bring mixture to a boil. As it cooks, it will become slightly thickened and creamy. Swirl the sauce while cooking to help maintain the texture and simmer until about half of the lemon juice is evaporated. Season sauce with salt and pepper to taste and stir in tarragon.

5. To serve, spread sweet potato mixture onto a serving platter. Arrange asparagus on top of sweet potatoes. Scatter the scallions on top of the asparagus. Top the scallions with chopped egg white and yolk. Spoon warm butter sauce over the top of the salad and serve.

Nothing completes a meal the way wine does. In fact, it doesn't feel like I'm eating a real dinner without a little wine to go with it.

Wine is a beverage that helps food be everything it can be without getting in its way. Adding wine to a meal instead of soft drinks or beer (though admittedly, beer does have its place) distinguishes it from other meals. But that shouldn't limit you from drinking it every day. Distinguishing a meal every day is a good idea. That said, I think there's far too much emphasis put on hard-to-find, expensive wines. There's so much good, reasonably priced, and widely available wine out there, there's no reason everyday dinners can't be special and distinguished. Those are the kinds of wines I chose to pair with the recipes in this book. They're all national brands that are about $20 a bottle (or less). They're all good people-pleasers—nothing too eccentric.

Every main-dish recipe (with the exception of those in the holiday chapter) is paired with at least one wine. Some recipes work with more than one wine, but none of them go without.

" Wine makes food taste better. It's that simple. This **WINE GUIDE** takes the guesswork out of pairing food with the perfect wine. **"**

PINOT GRIGIO
Borgo Conventi Pinot Grigio 2006 (Italy)

Coconut-Ginger Chicken Stir-Fry with Broccoli & Rice, p. 55

Salsa Verde Stir-Fried Chicken & Vegetables with Bacon, p. 70

Stir-Fry of Chicken with Hot & Sweet Peanut Sauce & Green Rice, p. 76

Broiled Chicken Thighs with Baba Ghanoush, Apricots & Cinnamon, p. 53

Linguine with Shrimp, Olives & Pepperoncini, p. 161

Orecchiette with Shrimp, Tomato & Sardines, p. 169

Spaghetti Tonnato, p. 164

Linguine with Clams & Bacon, p. 162

Mussel & Lentil Stew with Caponata & Pepperoni, p. 154

CHARDONNAY
Francis Ford Coppola Diamond Collection Chardonnay 2006 (California)

Chicken Alfredo, p. 187 ▼

Broiled Chicken Legs with Onions, Apples & Chunky Lemon-Pepper Sauce, p. 57

Grilled Turkey Steaks with Sautéed Belgian Endive, Bacon & Mango Chutney, p. 72

Roasted Butterflied Chicken with Shredded Potatoes, Onions & Thyme, p. 50

Rotisserie Chicken & Warm Bulgur Salad with Yogurt-Parsley Dressing, p. 62

Warm Chicken Salad with Tahini-Yogurt Dressing & Watercress, p. 63

Pork & Potato Dumplings with Creamy Smoked Paprika Sauce, p. 100

Smoked Pork Loin Medallions with Leek & Potato Stew, p. 108

Barbecue Salmon with Black Beans & Grits, p. 113

Fresh & Smoked Salmon Cakes with Chickpeas & Tangy Green Salad, p. 116

Salmon Filets with Tarragon Butter Sauce & Trevisano, p. 118

Clam & Corn Chowder with Potatoes & Bacon, p. 153

Shrimp & Lobster Stew with Corn & Zucchini, p. 145

Grilled Tuna Niçoise Salad, p. 132

Charred Chilean Sea Bass with Miso & Marmalade, p. 134

SAUVIGNON BLANC
Pouilly-Fumé 2007, Michele Redde (Loire Valley, France)

Chicken & Fresh Salsa Stew with Black Beans & Sour Cream, p. 183

Turkey Steaks with Sweet Potato, Roasted Almonds & Pomegranate Vinaigrette, p. 60

Fricassee of Boneless Chicken Thighs, Carrots, Raisins & Cumin, p. 68

Grilled Wasabi-Ginger Chicken Kebabs with Mushrooms & Lima Beans, p. 75

Spicy Szechuan Turkey, Carrot & Radicchio Stir-Fry, p. 67

Warm Chicken & Radicchio Salad with Orange, Tarragon & Goat Cheese, p. 78

Hot & Sour Pork Stew with Napa Cabbage, p. 88

Pork & Bok Choy Stir-Fry with Spicy Peanut Sauce, p. 97

Pork Enchiladas with Cheese & Tomatillo Salsa, p. 99

Pork Stir-Fry with Spicy Plum Sauce, Mustard
Greens & Rice, p. 107
Poached Salmon with Beets, Lemon & Broiled
String Beans, p. 180
Salmon in Tomato Gravy with Cubanelle Peppers &
Onions, p. 119
Salmon with Chili-Lime Marmalade, Red Peppers &
Water Chestnuts, p. 114
Hot Crab Louis Salad, p. 150
Scallops with Red Beans & Rice, p. 149
Shrimp au Poivre with Broiled Zucchini, p. 138
Shrimp Hash & Eggs, p. 142
Warm Shrimp & Potato Salad with Bacon, p. 147
Fresh Tuna Melts with Cheddar, Smoked Ham &
Mango Salsa, p. 128 ▲
Sesame Tuna Noodles, p. 127
Tuna & Tomato Crumble, p. 131
Popcorn Monkfish with Spicy Mayo, p. 135
Spicy Tuna Rolls & Mushroom Asparagus Rolls, p. 130

CABERNET SAUVIGNON
Relativity Vineyards 2005 (California)

Fettucine with Ribbons of Roast Beef, Artichokes &
Boursin, p. 167
Ground Beef with Red Cabbage & Sour
Cream, p. 19
Roast Beef with Teriyaki Rice Noodles & Scallions, p. 20
Pork Cordon Bleu with Chunky Mushroom
Sauce, p. 105
Sautéed Pork Cutlets with Apples, Collard Greens &
Bacon, p. 95
Beef Wellington, p. 26

MERLOT
Oxford Landing 2006 (Australia)

Curried Ground Beef & Noodle Stew
with Zucchini, p. 27
Quick Fricasee of Beef with Belgian Endive & Grape
Tomatoes, p. 40
Sweet & Sour Baked Chicken Tenders with
Trevisano, p. 77
Pork Cutlets with Snap Peas, Mushrooms &
Sherry, p. 98

ZINFANDEL
Dancing Bull 2005 (California)

Barbecue Roast Beef with Corn & Beans, p. 12
Grilled Beef Tenderloin with Noodles, Cashews & Chili
Sauce, p. 29
Stir-Fry of Beef with Black Beans, Red Peppers &
Broccoli, p. 41
Beef Tenderloin with Loaded Baked Yams, p. 189
Broiled Chicken Thighs with Stew of Mushrooms,
Corn & Cabbage, p. 54
Pork & Carrot Stew with Curry Lime & Cilantro
Broth, p. 93
Fried Pork & Beans, p. 89

Chicken & White Bean Soup with Spinach & Parmesan, p. 184
Mac 'n' Cheese with Shrimp, p. 141

TEMPRANILLO
Bodegas Arzuaga 'La Planta' Ribera del Duero 2007 (Spain)

Beef Tenderloin with Sweet & Sour Napa Cabbage, p. 13
Ground Beef with Cauliflower Curry & Rice, p. 37
Vietnamese Beef Salad, p. 47
Chicken & Chorizo Stew with Mustard Greens & Corn, p. 64
Chunky Pork & Pepper Pie with Puff Pastry, p. 86
Shrimp Paella with Chorizo, p. 143
Beef with Salsa Verde, Rice & Beans, p. 14

CÔTES DU RHÔNE
Patrick Lesec Côtes-du-Rhône 'Bouquet' 2005 (France)

Beef Tenderloin with Sweet & Sour Napa Cabbage, p. 13
Grilled Steak & Romaine with Peppers & Olives, p. 33
Boursin® & Ham-Stuffed Chicken with Couscous & Lentil Sauce, p. 52
Saffron-Scented Chicken Stew with Bacon & Artichokes, p. 66
Gruyère-Stuffed Pork with Garlicky Wild Mushrooms & Spinach, p. 90
Pork Chops Woodsman-Style with Potatoes, Peppers & Rosemary, p. 85
Pork Scaloppine with Mushroom & Red Wine Sauce, p. 103
Spicy Tuna with Couscous & Carrots, p. 179
Potato Gnocci with Wild Mushrooms, p. 173

SYRAH
Barrel 27 Central Coast 2005 (California)

Filet Mignon with Eggplant in Tangy Tomato Yogurt Sauce, p. 22
Grilled Ribeye with Warm Thai Peanut, Carrot & Snow Pea Slaw, p. 32
Moroccan Beef Stew, p. 34 ▲
Creamy Curried Pork & Zucchini with Crushed Chickpeas, p. 87
Jerk Pork Chops with Yams & Rice, p. 188
Spicy Tuna Rolls & Mushroom-Asparagus Rolls, p. 130

DOLCETTO
Dolcetto 'Fontanazza', Macarini 2006 (Italy)

Chopped Steak with Charred Onions & Queso Blanco, p. 24
Gingered Beef Stew with Bok Choy & Shiitake Mushrooms, p. 28
Grilled Beef Tenderloin & Pineapple au Poivre with Coconut Sauce, p. 11
Warm Roast Beef & Endive Salad with Peppers & Greek Yogurt, p. 44

INDEX

Note: Boldfaced page references indicate photographs.

Note: Boldfaced page references indicate photographs.

Note: Boldfaced page references indicate photographs.

Note: Boldfaced page references indicate photographs.

Note: Boldfaced page references indicate photographs.

Note: Boldfaced page references indicate photographs.

Note: Boldfaced page references indicate photographs.

Note: Boldfaced page references indicate photographs.

Note: Boldfaced page references indicate photographs.

Note: Boldfaced page references indicate photographs.

Acknowledgments

To my mother Nicolina, my father Raffaele, my sister Maria, and my brother Michael, for acting like I never make a mistake and thinking everything I do is flawless.

Linda Lisco, who unlike my family, makes sure to point out every mistake I make and always pushes me to be better. Can't blame her—it's her job. And she does it very well.

Michael Pedicone—who is that masked man?

Everyone at Meredith, who at breakneck pace put together another great book— especially Jan, Lisa, Mick, Kritsada, Ken, Erin, Jessica, Tricia, and Diana. Thanks also to Jeff, Amy, Ken, and Mike, for getting the word and the books out there!

Kris Kurek, who was my "recipe tester" on this book and my culinary producer for television—but who is so much more. She can cook like few can, read my mind, and somehow keep up with it all.

Everyone at Unilever, Bertolli, especially Brian, Christine, Russel, Jenn, Michael and Jeanine; our hero, Mark, and Rebecca, Patrick, and Gina, for creating a pinnacle life moment for me and including me in their fantastic plans.

Donyale McRae, who is a true master at his craft and who makes sure I feel good about myself when it counts.

Jim, Sandi, and teams for their stellar PR work and helping with all the moving parts!

All of my friends at NBC: Jeff, Ben, Craig, Meredith, and Jenny.

At Bravo: Lauren, Frances, Andy, Dave, Amy, and Eli.

At Reveille: Mark, Howard, Lee, and Chad.

At 3 Ball: JD and Todd.

The Magical Elves: Dan, Jane, and Shauna.

The producers of *The Today Show*: Alexandra, Dee Dee, Melissa.

Of *Top Chef*: Tom, Padma, Gail, Tim, and Ted—and the generous crew.

And T*he Biggest Loser*: Alison, Bob, Jillian, Cheryl, Carole, and the amazing contestants and crew.

The entire production crew of *Rocco Gets Rea*l. I thank them for their hard work and patience, even when we were finding our way. Thanks, too, to the great people we've cast on the show, for sharing their lives and homes with us.

And last but not least, to my good friends at A&E: Rob, Bob, Michael, Charles, Gina, Aimee, and Laurie, for making this possible. It's been a long journey, but we're finally here.

ROCCO DISPIRITO

What do you want to eat? Better yet, what do you want to cook?

In his cookbook, *Rocco's Real Life Recipes*, Chef Rocco DiSpirito offers more than 130 quick-to-fix main dishes built around totally accessible, everyday ingredients, short shopping lists and cooking times, and super-easy cleanup. He also includes "reserve" recipes for leisurely weekend cooking and recommendations for easy-to-find affordable wines for every recipe.

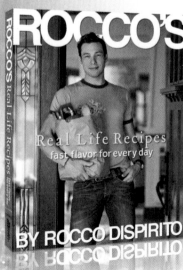

ROCCO'S Real Life Recipes
fast flavor for every day
BY ROCCO DISPIRITO